Poetry Prompt

MW00682968

Grades 4-6

Written by Ruth Solski
Illustrated by S&S Learning Materials

ISBN 1-55035-833-2
Copyright 2006
All Rights Reserved * Printed in Canada

Published in the United States by:
On the Mark Press
3909 Witmer Road PMB 175
Niagara Falls, New York
14305
www.onthemarkpress.com

Published in Canada by:
S&S Learning Materials
15 Dairy Avenue
Napanee, Ontario
K7R 1M4
www.sslearning.com

At A Glance™

Learning Expectations	Section 1	Section 2	Section 3	Section 4	Section 5	Section 6	Section 7	Section 8	Section 9	Section 10	Section 11	Section 12	Section 13	Section 14
Literacy Skills														
• Recognizing and identifying poetry forms	●				●	●	●	●	●	●	●	●	●	
• Learning about and implementing poetry forms					●	●	●	●	●	●	●	●	●	
• Developing choral reading skills		●												
• Developing poetry appreciation			●											
• Identifying the main idea		●	●											
• Understanding literary terms				●										
Creative Skills														
• Recognizing and Writing:														
• traditional poetry					●									
• rhyming couplets					●									
• rhyming triplets					●									
• quatrains					●									
• cinquains						●								
• acrostic poetry							●							
• limericks								●						
• haiku									●					
• alphabet										●				
• stair poetry											●			
• diamante												●		
• clerihew poetry													●	
• alliteration														●
• metaphors														●
• similes														●
• onomatopoeia														●

OTM-1875 • SSR1-75 Poetry Prompts

Table of Contents

Poetry Prompts

Teacher Assessment Rubric

Student's Name: _____

Criteria	Level 1	Level 2	Level 3	Level 4
Understanding Concepts	Demonstrates a limited understanding and interpretation of a poem	Demonstrates some understanding and interpretation of a poem	Demonstrates a general understanding and interpretation of a poem	Demonstrates a thorough understanding and interpretation of a poem
Critical Analysis & Appreciation	Analyzes and describes a poem with assistance	Analyzes and describes a poem with some assistance	Analyzes and describes a poem with little assistance	Analyzes and describes a poem independently
Identification of Poetry Forms	Identifies poetry forms with assistance	Identifies poetry forms with some assistance	Identifies poetry forms with little assistance	Identifies poetry forms readily with no assistance
Following a Poetry Outline	Follows a poetry outline with assistance	Follows a poetry outline with some assistance	Follows poetry outline with little assistance	Follows a poetry outline independently
Creative Expression	Expresses ideas creatively with assistance	Expresses ideas creatively with some assistance	Expresses ideas creatively with little assistance	Expresses ideas creatively with no assistance
Choral Reading	Reads poetry expressively with assistance	Reads poetry expressively with some assistance	Reads poetry expressively with little assistance	Reads poetry expressively independently
Poetry Appreciation	Shows little interest in poetry	Shows some interest in poetry	Shows good interest in poetry	Enjoys and reads poetry often

Comments:

_____

_____

_____

Poetry Prompts

Student Self-Assessment Rubric

Name: _____

Put a check mark in the box that best describes your performance and feelings. Then, add your points to determine your total score.

Expectations	My Performance				My Points
	Always (4 points)	Almost Always (3 points)	Sometimes (2 points)	Needs Improvement (1 point)	
✓ I listen well, follow directions and remain on task during each poetry lesson.	✓				4 / 4
✓ I understand the ideas that a poet expresses in his/her poetry.	✓	✓			8 / 4
✓ I enjoy participating with a group chorally reading poetry.		✓			10 / 3
✓ I am able to express my ideas using different forms of poetry.	✓				15 / 4
✓ I revise and edit my work and make corrections.			✓	✓	16 / 4
✓ I enjoy listening to different forms of poetry read aloud.	✓				20 / 3

Total Points: 22

Introduction

Poetry is a type of literature in which the sound and meaning of language are combined to create ideas and feelings. In today's society, poetry is everywhere. It is found in the lyrics of songs, heard in television commercials, radio jingles, written in greeting cards and said in jump rope chants.

People are attracted by the sound and rhythm of a poem's words. Poetry comes in different shapes and sizes. Poems are filled with feelings, ideas, moods, topics and stories. Children enjoy the pleasing rhythms found in nursery rhymes. They will clap their hands and move their bodies to the rhythm of the language.

Poetry began in prehistoric times. Poetic language was used by early people in songs, prayers and magic spells. The pattern of rhyme and rhythm helped people to remember and preserve oral poetry from generation to generation. After writing was developed, people were able to record their poetry and it became an important art form. In the world today, millions of people listen to, or read poetry. Many people also write it.

Kinds of Poetry

There are three main kinds of poetry. They are lyric, narrative and dramatic.

Lyric poetry is the most common type. The word 'lyric' comes from 'lyre', a harplike musical instrument, played by ancient Greek poets while they recited their short poems. Lyric poetry means any short poem.

The haiku is a form of Japanese poetry and is the shortest type of lyric poetry. The haiku consists of 17 syllables written in three lines. The first line has 5 syllables, the second 7, and the third 5.

The sonnet is a 14 line lyric poem with a certain pattern of rhyme and rhythm. Many sonnets are love poems.

Epics and ballads are narrative poems because they tell a story. Epics are the longest poems that describe the deeds of heroes in battle or conflicts between human beings and natural and divine forces. Some epics tell of the origin or the history of a people. Epics are the oldest form of poetry that have survived throughout the centuries. The Illiad and the Odyssey are two of the most famous epics in Western literature and were written during the 700's B.C.. The Illiad describes the events that took place in the last year of the Trojan War, which was fought between Greece and the city of Troy. The epic called the Odyssey, tells of the adventures of Odysseus, King of Ithaca, on his return home from the Trojan War.

Ballads tell stories about a particular person. These stories are shorter than epics. There are many ballads written about the adventures of Robin Hood, a legendary outlaw who stole from the rich and gave to the poor.

Section 1

Poetry Writing Stimulators

Students often have no appreciation or understanding of the art form called poetry. They will moan and groan at the mere mention of the word. Students must be exposed to all forms of poetry writings well before they try to write. Poetry must be enjoyed and appreciated as a skillfully written art form. According to Ruskin reading poetry is like the erecting of fairy palaces of magic thought, proof against all adversity. To learn in school to love poetry helps to build such palaces and desires.

Often teachers shy away from implementing poetry writing because they have no idea where to begin or how to stimulate interest in it. Listed below are some ways to help the classroom teacher to stimulate interest and to promote this art form.

1. Read at least one poem each day, perhaps just before recess or before dismissal time. Reread old favorites as well. Frequent reading will often commit the poem to memory so encourage the class to "join in" as you read.

2. Poetry should be readily accessible, taped or printed on index cards. The 5" x 8" cards seem best for a collection. Organize the cards as to theme, seasons, special days or author.

3. Use a poem to center a bulletin board display. The poem of the month might be surrounded with related pictures of student art.

4. Poems printed or written on chart paper may be displayed on classroom doors with related pictures.

5. Display poetry on window ledges, shelf tops, banners that hang, or at an interest center.

   a) on a series of connected cards:

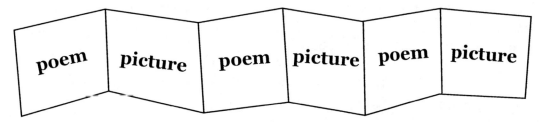

   b) in a file folder or Bristol Board folder with a related picture and/or an assignment:

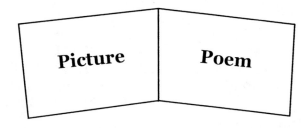

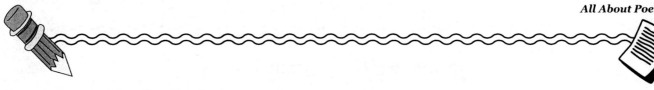

c) on cards with related picture:

Picture	Poem

6. Include anthologies of poems at the library corner. Encourage students to write or print their own favorite poems in a workbook with related illustrations.

7. Introduce the writing of poetry by reading and displaying many examples of the following poetic forms.

Nursery Rhymes	Haiku Poems
Rhyming Couplets	Alphabet Poems
Quatrains	Alliteration
Cinquains	Name Poems
Limericks	Diamantes
Stair poems	Clerihew
Shape Poems	Ballad
Terse Verse	

8. Poetry is one short easy-to-read written format that appeals to reluctant readers. Include many short poems (four to eight lines) with jokes and riddles when selecting material for individualized reading.

9. Use poetry selections as part of your reading program with open-ended activities to be completed after the reading of a poem. Poems pertaining to special celebrations and events would work well in this type of activity.

10. Focus on the work of one poet. Read several of his/her poems and present them on charts or cards for a bulletin board display. The following writers are popular with students at the junior level.

Dennis Lee	Kaye Starbird
Shel Silverstein	Eve Merrian
David McCord	John Ciardi
Carl Sandburg	Mary O'Neill
Raymond Souster	Jack Prelutsky
Gene Fehier	Bruce Lansky
Robert Frost	

Section 1

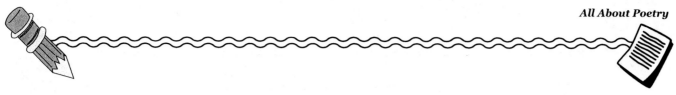

11. Here are different ways of presenting a poetry lesson.

   a) Read three or four ballads of differing moods. Brief comments or questions can pinpoint the differences and similarities.
   b) Read five or six poems (depending on their length) all by the same author. Bring him to life with a few biographical details. A picture of the poet is a welcomed addition to the lesson.
   c) Read four or five poems on the same subject which express different attitudes.
   d) Let several children each choose a poem from an anthology and read it aloud in turn to the class, having practiced before hand. Then briefly discuss similarities and differences between the choices. If this activity is repeated throughout the year, each student in the class will have an opportunity to take part.
   e) Have a choral reading presentation by the students of a dramatic poem. Choose one with refrains and choruses.
   f) Have a brief request session in the last few minutes of a lesson or devote a whole lesson to reading again favorites from the preceding weeks lessons.
   g) A good way to begin in the fall is to read poems written by Shel Silverstein from the book "Where the Sidewalk Ends". They form an excellent introductory unit for the fall term. Junior level (Grades 4 to 6) students are fond of humorous poets. Read the following poems:

Merry	For Sale
The Planet of Mars	The Gypsies Are Coming
The Loser	Pirate Captain Jim
Melinda Mae	

12. Create a Poetry Writing Center or Corner in your classroom.

   a) Place a table near a bulletin board or in a private area. Label the center in an interesting fashion e.g. Poet's Center, Poet's Corner, I'm a Poet and Didn't Know It. Poetry writing Center, etc. Display student poetry in an attractive manner.
   b) Place paper, pencils, pens, erasers, marking pens, pencil crayons, glue, dictionary, thesaurus, word family lists, rhyming word lists and task cards.
   c) Make up task cards and place them in small manilla envelopes. Pin the envelopes to the bulletin board.
   d) Students will select a task card and then write this type of poem described on the card.
   e) The poems written could be read to the class if the author chooses to do so.

14. Poetry written by the students could be recorded in Classroom Poetry Books, School Magazines, School Newspapers and Poetry Books for the resource center (library).

Choral Reading

Choral reading is as old as poetry itself. It was one of the earliest forms of artistic expression used during festivals and religious rites of primitive people before it was used in the presentation of dramatic ideas in the theater. It is still used today for ritualistic purposes in congregational reading of psalms and other liturgical literature in church worship.

Choral reading is a delightful way for students to read aloud poetry in school. At the same time it will develop an appreciation of different forms of poetry as well as promote and strengthen reading with expression. This type of group reading provides a unique social experience shared by all students.

Classroom Choral Reading

1. Select a poem that your students will be able to read and memorize easily. Look for one with a catchy title that will put imaginations to work. Some of Shel Silverstein's poetry would work well with the students for choral readings. The poem would come alive when read aloud. The words should be fascinating and there should be a contrast of some sort that can be interpreted. The mood of the poem is easily enhanced through oral interpretations.

2. Record the poem on chart paper, the chalk board, an overhead or on a reproducible handout.

3. Read the poem aloud to the students with good expression and clear enunciation. Use your pointer or hand to demonstrate the flow and rhythm as you read.

4. Discuss the topic, mood and descriptive vocabulary, punctuation or lack of it.

5. Read the poem again and have your students hand clap or tap their foot to feel the rhythm.

6. Read the poem with the entire class, several times to feel the rhythm together.

7. Next comes the fun! There are a number of possibilities to develop the poem into a choral reading piece. Try to select the most appropriate voice elements to reinforce the meaning of the selection. Contrast is the key to success. Use one or two simple classifications for the voices such as high, low as well as strong and soft. Try some of the suggested strategies listed below.

   a) Alternate slow and fast lines.
   b) Alternate soft and loud lines.
   c) Alternate low and high voices.
   d) Emphasize key words and phrases by reading them in a louder or softer voice.
   e) Pause for a specified number of "beats" before you join in and continue reading.
   f) Clap or make a certain sound at the end of certain lines.

g) The solo device in choral reading serves two specific purposes. First, it provides for the first personal pronoun or what would be the speaker himself.

Example: **Whistle**

I want to learn to whistle *(Solo 1)*
I've always wanted to; *(Solo 2)*
I fix my mouth to do it, but *(All)*
The whistle won't come through. *(All)*

I think perhaps it's stuck and so *(Solo 3)*
I try it once again *(Solo 3)*
Can people swallow whistles? *(All)*
Where is my whistle then? *(All)*

Anonymous

The solo is also used to call attention to each of the following factors:

1. the meaning of a particular line
2. the abrupt introduction of a new idea or thought
3. the expression of a subdued word
4. a phrase
5. a sentence
6. deep feeling
7. mock-seriousness
8. the best possible means to give a number of different individual students an opportunity to participate in an important function of reading

Poetry Selections for Choral Reading

Do the following old Nursery Rhymes, for fun with your class to get them into the swing of enjoying reading chorally.

A Farmer Went Riding

A farmer went riding upon his gray mare, *(Girls)*
Bumpety, bumpety, bump! *(Boys)*
With his daughter behind him, so rosy and fair *(Girls)*
Lumpety, lumpety, lump! *(Boys)*

A raven cried "croak"! *(Solo)* and they all tumbled down, *(All)*
Bumpety, bumpety, bump! *(Boys)*
The mare broke her knees and the farmer his crown, *(Girls)*
Lumpety, lumpety, lump! *(Boys)*

Section 2

The mischievous raven flew laughing away, *(Boys)*
Bumpety, bumpety, bump! *(Girls)*
And wowed he would serve them the same the next day, *(Boys)*
Humpety, humpety, hump. *(All)*

Mary Had a Little Lamb

Solo 1:	Mary had a little lamb,
Girls:	Its fleece was white as snow;
All:	And everywhere that Mary went,
All:	The lamb was sure to go.

Boys:	He followed her to school one day,
Solo 2:	Which was against the rule,
Boys:	It made the children laugh and play
Girls:	To see a lamb at school.

Solo 3:	And so the teacher turned him out,
Girls:	But still he lingered near,
All:	And waited patiently about
All:	Till Mary did appear.

Solo 4:	Then, he ran to her, and laid
All:	His head upon her arm,
Solo 5:	As if he said, "I'm not afraid –
All:	You'll keep me from all harm."

All:	"What makes the lamb love Mary so?"
All:	The eager children cry.
Solo 6:	"Oh Mary loves the lamb, you know,"
All:	The teacher did reply.

Girls:	And you each gentle animal
Girls:	In confidence may bind,
Boys:	And make them follow at your will,
All:	If you are only kind.

Sing A Song of Sixpence

All:	Sing a song of sixpence,
All:	A pocket full of rye,
Girls:	Four and twenty blackbirds
All:	Baked in a pie;
Boys:	When the pie was opened,
Boys:	The birds began to sing;
All:	Wasn't that a dainty dish

Section 2

All:	To set before the King?
Boys:	The king was in the counting-house
Boys:	Counting out his money;
Girls:	The queen was in the parlor
Girls:	Eating bread and honey;
Solo 1:	The maid was in the garden
All:	Hanging out the clothes,
Solo 2:	Along came a blackbird,
All:	And snapped off her nose.

Anonymous

Song of the Witches

Solo 1:	Double, double, toil and trouble;
Solo 2:	Fire burn and cauldron bubble.
Boys:	Fillet of a fenny snake,
Boys:	In the caldron boil and bake;
Girls:	Eye of newt and toe of frog,
Girls:	Wool of bat and tongue of dog,
All:	Adder's fork and blind-worm's sting.
All:	Lizard's leg and howlet's wing,
Solo 1:	For a charm of powerful trouble,
Solo 2:	Like a hell-broth boil and bubble.
All:	Double, double, toil and trouble;
All:	Fire burn and cauldron bubble.
Solo 1:	Cool it with a baboon's blood,
Solo 2:	Then the charm is firm and good.

Poor Old Lady

All:	Poor old lady, she swallowed a fly,
Solo 1:	I don't know why she swallowed a fly.
Boys:	Poor old lady, I think she'll die.
All:	Poor old lady, she swallowed a spider
Solo 1:	It squirmed and wiggled and turned inside her.
Solo 2:	She swallowed the spider to catch the fly.
Solo 2:	I don't know why she swallowed a fly.
Girls:	Poor old lady, I think she'll die.
All:	Poor old lady, she swallowed a bird.
Solo 1:	How absurd! She swallowed a bird.
Solo 2:	She swallowed the bird to catch the spider,

Section 2

Solo 3:	She swallowed the spider to catch the fly.
All:	I don't know why she swallowed a fly.
All:	Poor old lady, I think she'll die.

All:	Poor old lady, she swallowed a cat.
Solo 1:	Think of that! She swallowed a cat.
Solo 2:	She swallowed the cat to catch the bird.
Solo 3:	She swallowed the bird to catch the spider.
Solo 4:	She swallowed the spider to catch the fly,
All:	I don't know why she swallowed a fly.
All:	Poor old lady, I think she'll die.

All:	Poor old lady, she swallowed a dog.
Solo 1:	She went the whole hog when she swallowed the dog.
Solo 2:	She swallowed the dog to catch the cat,
Solo 3:	She swallowed the cat to catch the bird,
Solo 4:	She swallowed the bird to catch the spider.
Solo 5:	She swallowed the spider to catch the fly,
All:	I don't know why she swallowed a fly.
All:	Poor old lady, I think she'll die.

All:	Poor old lady, she swallowed a cow.
Solo 1:	I don't know how she swallowed the cow.
Solo 2:	She swallowed the cow to catch the dog,
Solo 3:	She swallowed the dog to catch the cat,
Solo 4:	She swallowed the cat to catch the bird,
Solo 5:	She swallowed the bird to catch the spider
Solo 6:	She swallowed the spider to catch the fly.
All:	I don't know why she swallowed a fly
All:	Poor old lady, I think she'll die.

Solo 7:	Poor old lady, she swallowed a horse.
All:	She died, of course.

Anonymous

The Three Little Pigs

All:	Once upon a time in a tale often told,
	There lived three pigs who were little and bold.
Trio:	"Oh mother dear, we find this house much too small,
(Pigs)	It is not big enough to hold us all.
Trio:	We want to go out and look on our own,
(Pigs)	For a new place to build our homes."

Section 2

Boys: Their mother warned of a wolf bad and big,
                 Who especially liked to eat fat pink pigs.

Girls: Off they went in three different ways,
                 Over the land they traveled for days.

Boys: The three little pigs built their homes real quick,
                 They used every straw, stick and brick.

All: They lived happily in their new homes for awhile,
                 They had not seen the wolf hiding and watching with a smile.

Girls: One day the wolf walked up to the house of straw,
Boys: He knocked and he knocked on the door with his paw.

Solo: Little pig, little pig, you'd better let me come in!
(Wolf)   Or I'll huff and I'll puff and I'll blow your house in.

Trio: Oh no – squealed the pig – By the hair on my chin
(Pigs)   I'll never, never, never, never let you in.

All: The wolf gave a huff, and a puff or two,
                 The house began to fall as he blew;
                 It shook first one way, then the other,
                 So the pig ran off to visit his brother.

Girls: The wolf strode up to the house of wood,
                 He knocked and he knocked as loud as he could.

Solo: Little pigs, he called, you'd better let me in,
(Wolf)   Or I'll huff and puff and I'll blow your house in.

Trio: Oh no! squealed the pigs – By the hair on each chin,
(Pigs)   We'll never, never, never, never let you in.

All: The wolf gave a huff and a puff or two,
                 The house began to fall as he blew and blew.
                 It shook first one way, then the other,
                 So the pigs ran off to visit their brother.

Boys: The wolf strode up to the house of brick,
                 He knocked on the door with a great big stick.

Solo: Little pigs, he called, you'd better let me in,
(Wolf)   Or I'll huff and I'll puff and I'll blow your house in.

Trio: Oh, no! squealed the pigs – By the hair on each chin,

Section 2

All: The wolf gave a huff and a puff or two
           But the house wouldn't fall though he blew and blew,
           He huffed and he puffed the whole day long
           But the house of brick stood firm and strong.
           The wolf climbed up to the roof top brown,
           He strode to the chimney and he shouted down.

Solo: Little pigs, he cried, Just open the door,
(Wolf)   Or I'll slide down the chimney till I reach the floor.

Trio: Come, on squealed the pigs as they poked up the fire.
(Pigs)   And the water in the pot bubbled higher and higher.

Solo: Here I come, cried the wolf and down he slid;
(Wolf)

All: He landed in the pot and the pigs put on the lid.
           They cooked him there in the boiling bubbles,
           And that was the end of the little pigs' troubles.

Anonymous

Wolf: Gruff Voice
Pigs: High Pitched Voices

Poetry Appreciation

In order to develop a love and an appreciation for poetry, students should be exposed to it on a regular basis in an interesting and subtle manner. Poetry should be written on charts, reproducible handouts, overheads or on a chalkboard so that it is highly visible. The poems should be read for enjoyment and at the same time attention is drawn to how poetry is read. Read the poem to the students in an enthusiastic way, varying your voice tones and pausing at significant punctuation marks. Note where punctuation marks are located and the absence of the marks. Instruct your students to continue to the next line without pausing if there isn't a punctuation mark. If one is at the end of a line, there should be a slight pause before reading the next line. Discuss the interesting vocabulary and the ways the poet has made the poem interesting. Have the students indicate the type of voice tones they could use while reading the poem. Chorally read the poem again with your students indicating the flow and rhythm with your hand or a pointer. This exercise will improve and strengthen oral reading skills while developing good expression. Explain to your students that reading a poem is like singing a song only you are saying the words.

Write any of the following poems on a chart or an overhead.

Section 2

Two Little Kittens

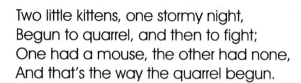

Two little kittens, one stormy night,
Begun to quarrel, and then to fight;
One had a mouse, the other had none,
And that's the way the quarrel begun.

"I'll have that mouse," said the biggest cat;
"You'll have that mouse? We'll see about that!"
"I will have that mouse," said the eldest son;
"You shan't have the mouse," said the little one.
I told you before 'twas a stormy night;
When these two little kittens began to fight;
The old woman seized her sweeping broom,
And swept the kittens right out of the room.

The ground was covered with frost and snow,
And the two little kittens had no where to go;
So they laid them down on the mat at the door,
While the old woman finished sweeping the floor.
Then they crept in, as quiet as mice,
All wet with snow, and cold as ice,
For they found it was better, that stormy night,
To lie down and sleep than to quarrel and fight.

Author Unknown

The Months of the Year

January brings the snow,
Makes our feet and fingers glow.
February brings the rain,
Thaws the frozen lake again.
March brings breezes loud and shrill,
Stirs the dancing daffodil.
April brings the primrose sweet,
Scatters daisies at our feet.
May brings flocks of pretty lambs,
Skipping by their fleecy dams.
June brings tulips, lilies, roses,
Fills the children's hands with posies.

Section 3

Hot July brings cooling showers,
Apricots and gilly flowers.
August brings the sheaves of corn,
Then the harvest home is borne.
Warm September brings the fruit,
Sportsmen then begin to shoot.
Fresh October brings the pheasant,
Then to gather nuts is pleasant.
Dull November brings the blast,
Then the leaves are whirling fast.
Chill December brings the sleet,
Blazing fire and Christmas treat.

Anonymous

Smart

My dad gave me one dollar bill
'Cause I'm his smartest son,
And I swapped it for two shiny quarters
'Cause two is more than one!
And then I took the quarters
And traded then to Lou
For three dimes – I guess he don't know
That three is more than two.

Just then, along came old blind Bates
And just 'cause he can't see
He gave me four nickels for my three dimes,
And four is more than three!

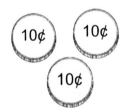

And I took the nickels to Hiram Coombs
Down at the seed-feed store,
And the fool gave me five pennies for them,
And five is more than four!

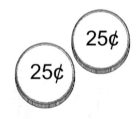

And then I went and showed my dad,
And he got red in the cheeks
And closed his eyes and shook his head –
Too proud of me to speak!

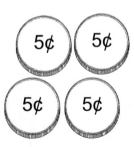

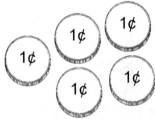

Anonymous

Falling Snow

See the pretty snowflakes
Falling from the sky;
On the walk and housetop
Soft and thick they lie.

On the window-ledges
On the branches bare,
Now how fast they gather
Filling all the air.

Looking into the garden,
Where the grass was green;
Covered by the snowflakes,
Not a blade is seen.

Now the bare black bushes
All look soft and white,
Every twig is laden –
What a pretty sight!

Anonymous

A Funful Night

When black cats howl
And pumpkins glare
And witches ride
The midnight air,
When crisp leaves crackle
On the ground
And tip toe feet
Are heard around
When lone owl hoots
And houses creak
When brownies play
At hide and seek,
Then turn yourself
Into a sprite
And come abroad –
That funful night –

Anonymous

Section 3

The Owl

In an oak liv'd an owl,
Frisky, whisky, wheedle!
She thought herself a clever fowl;
Fiddle, faddle, feedle.

Her face alone her wisdom shew,
Frisky, whisky, wheedle!
For all she said was, Whit te whoo!
Fiddle, faddle, feedle.

Her silly note a gunner heard,
Frisky, whisky, wheedle!
Says he, I'll shoot you, stupid bird!
Fiddle, faddle, feedle.

Anonymous

A Secret

Pussy Willow had a secret
That a snowdrop told to her,
And she purred it to the south wind,
While it stroked her velvet fur.
And the south wind hummed it softly
To the busy honeybees,
And they buzzed it to the blossoms
On the scarlet maple trees.
And they told it to the wood brooks
Brimming full of melted snow,
And the brooks told Robin Redbreast
As he chattered to and fro.
Little Robin could not keep it,
So he sang it loud and clear,
To the sleepy hills and meadows,
"Wake up! Cheer Up ! Spring is here."

Anonymous

Section 3

The Owl and the Pussy – Cat

The Owl and the Pussy-cat went to sea
In a beautiful pea-green boat:
They took some honey, and plenty of money
Wrapped up in a five-pound note.
The Owl looked up to the stars above,
And sang to a small guitar,
"O lovely Pussy, O Pussy, My love,
What a beautiful Pussy you are,
You are,
You are!
What a beautiful Pussy you are!"

Pussy said to the Owl, "You elegant fowl,
How charmingly sweet you sing!
Oh! let us be married; too long we have tarried:
But what shall we do for a ring?"
They sailed away, for a year and a day,
To the land where the Bong-tree grows;
And there in a wood a Piggy-wig stood,
With a ring at the end of his nose,
His nose,
His nose,
With a ring at the end of his nose.

"Dear Pig, are you willing to sell for one shilling
Your ring?" Said the Piggy, "I will."
So they took it away, and were married next day
By the Turkey who lives on the hill.
They dined on mince and slices of quince,
Which they ate with a runcible spoon;
And hand in hand, on the edge of the sand,
They danced by the light of the moon,
The moon,
The moon,
They danced by the light of the moon.

Edward Lear

Windy Nights

Whenever the moon and stars are set,
Whenever the wind is high,
All night long in the dark and wet
A man goes riding by.
Late in the night when the fires are, out
Why does he gallop and gallop about?

Whenever the trees are crying aloud,
And ships are tossed at sea,
By on the highway low and loud,
By at the gallop goes he.
By at the gallop he goes, and then
By he comes back at the gallop again.

Robert L. Stevenson

Gray and White

There was once a rabbit with silver fur;
Her little gray neighbors looked up to her,
Til she thought with pride in the moon-lit wood,
"The reason I'm white is because I'm good."

"Oh what shall I do? cried a tiny mole;
A fairy has tumbled into a hole;
It's full of water and crawling things,
And she can't get out, for she's hurt her wings.

"I did my best to catch hold of her,
But my arms are so short, and she's still in there,
Oh! darling white rabbit, your arms are long,
You say you are good and I know you are strong."

"Don't tell me about it," the rabbit said, –
She shut up her eyes and her ears grew red; –
"There's lot's of mud, and it's sure to stick,
Because my hair is so long and thick."

"Oh dear! Oh dear! sobbed the poor little mole,
Who will help the fairy out of the hole?"
A common gray rabbit popped up from the gorse.
"I'm not very strong, but I'll try, of course."

His little tail bobbed as he waded in,
The muddy water came up to his chin,
But he caught the fairy tight by the hand
And sent her off safe into Fairy-land.

But she kissed him first on his muddy nose,
She kissed his face, and his little wet toes,
And when the day dawned, in the early light
That little white rabbit was shining white.

Anonymous

Mr. Nobody

I know a funny little man,
As quiet as a mouse,
Who does the mischief that is done
In everybody's house!
There's no one ever sees his face,
And yet we all agree
That every plate we break was cracked
By Mr. Nobody.

'Tis he who always tears our books,
Who leaves the door ajar;
And scatters pins afar;
That squeaking door will always squeak
For, prithee, don't you see,
We leave the oiling to be done
By Mr. Nobody.

He puts damp wood upon the fire,
That kettles cannot boil;
His are the feet that bring in mud,
And all the carpets soil.
The papers always are mislaid,
Who had them last but he?
There's no one tosses them about
But Mr. Nobody.

The finger marks upon the door
By none of us are made;
We never leave the blinds unclosed,
To let the curtains fade.
The ink we never spill, the boots
That lying round you see
Are not our boots; they all belong
To Mr. Nobody.

Anonymous

Section 3

Further your students' appreciation and enjoyment of good poetry by including the following poems written by recognized authors.

Author	Poetry
Eve Merriam	Souvenir Metaphor A Spell of Weather A Vote for Vanilla Exploring Pandora's Box
Aileen Fisher	Wearing of the Green Firsting Voices in the Sky The Wind of Fall Zero Weather Feather Stitching Frosty White Shelling Peas Light in the Darkness
Eleanor Farjeon	V is for Vanilla Pole-Star A Dragon Fly Pencil and Paint
Dorothy Aldus	Wasps Every Insect
Shel Siverstein	Boa Constrictor Sarah Cynthia Stout Would Not Take the Garbage Out My Rules The Unicorn
Mary O'Neill	North Wind What is Yellow?
Dennis Lee	Tricking In Kamloops
Vicki McIntosh	Autumn
Kaye Starbird	The Leaf Pile

Author	Poetry
James S. Tippitt	Silent Storm Sleet Storm
Don Marquis	The Flattered Lightning Bug
Carl Sandburg	Summer Grass Fog
Charlotte Zolotow	Summer Snow
Kathryn Jackson	Things of Summer
Don Marshall	Cookout
Karla Kuskin	Said in Summer The Witches' Ride
Vicki McIntosh	Autumn
David McCord	Trick or Treat
Jack Prelutsky	Wild Witches Ball
Solveig Paulson Russell	Ants Cricket Song
Ethel Jacobson	Flies
Elsee Lingden	Beetles in the Garden
Conrad Aiden	The Grasshopper
Margaret Hillert	Tracks in the Snow
Rachel Field	Snow in the City
Ogden Nash	Winter Morning
Kaye Starbird	Eat-It-All-Elaine
Anne McCune	Food
Michael Vallins	The Night the Kitchen Came Alive
C.J. Erickson	Speaking of Eggs
Eunice Tietjens	Old Maps
Annette Wynne	Columbus

Poetry Definitions

The following terms are often used while referring to the reading and the writing of poetry.

alliteration – the repetition of the beginning sound or letter in two or more words in a line of verse. **Example:** "Peter Piper picked a peck of pickled peppers."

assonance – is the repetition of vowel sounds with varying consonant sounds. **Example:** "mine" and "night" have assonance of "i" sounds.

consonance – is the repetition of consonant sounds anywhere in a word in a line of verse. **Example:** Simple Simon met a pie man going to the fair.

couplet – is a pair of rhyming lines that contain one idea.

end rhyme – occurs when words rhyme at the end of two or more lines. **Example:** One, two, three, four five, Once I caught a fish alive.

foot – is a metrical unit of two or more syllables.

internal rhyme – is the rhyming of words within a line of poetry. **Example:** Little Bo-Peep has lost her sheep.

metaphor – compares two different things as if they were the same without using the words such as "like" or "as". **Example:** The sun is a fiery ball that moves from east to west in the sky.

meter – is the pattern of the rhythm in a poem

onomatopoeia – is a word whose sound suggests the sound to which it refers. **Example:** buzz, growl, screech, hiss, swishes

quatrain – is a four line stanza or line poem. The rhyme scheme varies.
      Example: a-a-a-a, a-b-a-b, a-b-c-d, a-a-b-b

repetition – is the repeating of a word, phrase or sounds to provide emphasis or rhythm.

rhyme – takes place when two or more words have the same or similar sounds.

rhyme scheme – is the pattern of rhyme in a poem. If the first and third lines in a quatrain rhyme, its rhyming scheme is a-b-a-b. If all four lines in a quatrain rhyme, its rhyming scheme is a-a-a-a. If the second and fourth lines rhyme in a quatrain the rhyming scheme is a-b-c-b.

simile – is a comparison of two things using such words as "like" or "as".
      Example: He is as fat as a pig.

stanza – is a group of lines in a poem. The couplet is a two line stanza, the triplet is a three line stanza and the quatrain is a four line stanza.

verse – is a line of traditional poetry written in meter. A verse is named after the number of feet it has per line. **Example:** one foot – manometer; two feet – dimeter; three feet – trimeter; four feet – tetrameter; five feet – pentameter; six feet – hexameter; seven feet – heptameter; eight feet – octometer.

Traditional Poetry

Traditional poetry is recognized readily because it is the most frequently seen form. It follows certain patterns of rhyme and rhythm.

Read the following poem. Note the rhyme scheme used. The lines that rhyme are marked with the same letter.

Grasshopper Green

Grasshopper Green is a comical chap	a
He lives on the best of fare.	b
Bright little trousers, jacket, and cap,	a
These are his summer wear.	b
Out in the meadow he loves to go,	c
Playing away in the sun;	d
It's hopperty, skipperty, high and low,	c
Summer's the time for fun.	d

A traditional poem has meter or rhythm. This is what you hear when you read the poem. Clap your hands while you read the poem about "Grasshopper Green". Can you feel its rhythm?

Read the following poems. Clap the rhythm. Mark the rhyming scheme.

If

If all the world was apple-pie,
And all the sea was ink,
And all the trees were bread and cheese
What would we have to drink?

Ten Little Mice

Ten little mice sat down to spin,
Pussy passed by and she looked in:
"What are you doing, my fine little men?"
"We're making coats for gentlemen."
"Shall I come in and bite your threads?"
"Oh, no Mistress Pussy; you'd bite off our heads

Section 5

Traditional Poetry

Nursery rhymes are poems that are often read to young children because of their rhyme and rhythm.

How well do you remember the early poems of your childhood?

Complete each rhyme with its missing words.

Little Miss _CAT_ Sat on a _MAT_, Eating her curds and _____, Along came a _____, Who sat down _____ _____, And frightened Miss Muffet _____.	"Pussy- _oh_ _____, Pussy- _____, Where have you _been_ ?" I've been to _every city near_ To look at the _time_ . "Pussy- _____, Pussy- _____, What did you _____?" "I frightened a little _____ Under the _____.
Little Boy Blue, come, blow your _____! The Sheep's in the meadow, the cow's in the _____. Where's the little boy that looks after the _____? Under the haystack fast _____!	Rain, rain, go _____, Come again another _____; Little Johnny wants to _____.
Georgy Porgy, pudding and _____, Kissed the girls and made them _____. When the boys came out to _____, Georgy Porgy ran _____.	Little Jack _____ Sat in the _____, Eating his Christmas _____: He put in his _____, And pulled out a _____, And said, "What a good boy am _____!"

Choose one of the nursery rhymes from above. Use it as a pattern to write your own nursery rhyme.

Section 5

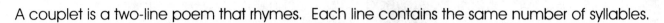

Rhyming Couplets

A couplet is a two-line poem that rhymes. Each line contains the same number of syllables.

Example:
> Twenty froggies went to school
> Down beside a rushy pool.

Complete the rhyming couplets with a word that rhymes with the last word of the first line.

1. Although Jack Frost could not be seen
   Our garden is no longer _____ .

2. As I look through the window pane
   I like to watch the falling _____ .

3. On the way to school today
   Eric saw a red fox at _____ .

4. All along the road to school
   There was ice on every _____ .

5. Did you have a chance to see
   The baby squirrels playing in the _____ ?

6. The dog was crawling on the ground
   The bone he lost could not be _____ .

7. At evening when I go to bed
   I see the stars shinning _____ .

8. "Come little leaves," said the wind one day
   "Come o'er the meadows with me and _____ .

9. Melissa lived in a little white house
   With a little black kitten and a little gray _____ .

10. The little flowers came through the ground,
    They raise their heads and looked _____ .

11. I wonder where all the rabbits go
    Who leave their tracks across the _____ .

12. Ten white pigeons are standing in line,
    On the roof of the barn in the warm _____ .

Rhyming Couplets

A couplet is a two-line poem that rhymes. Each line contains the same number of syllables.

Example: We have a secret, just we three, –
The robin and I and the cherry tree.

Compose rhymes of two lines by adding a line to each of these first lines.

1. The dog was crawling on the ground,

_____

2. The one who's it will look around,

_____

3. After the football game I went to bed,

_____

4. Most living things go out of sight,

_____

5. On wings of gold I'd like to fly,

_____

6. When you go out to play a game,

_____

7. When I saw the moon last night,

_____

8. When the snow comes down on me,

_____

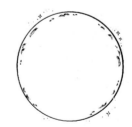

9. The rain on my cheeks was fresh and cool,

_____

10. The train rumbled loudly over the tracks,

_____

11. One night as I walked through the wood,

_____

12. When the earth has turned to spring,

_____

Section 5

Writing Rhyming Couplets

Remember – a rhyming couplet is a two line poem that rhymes at the end of the lines.

In the box below you will find pairs of rhyming words

town	fish	dream	high
clown	dish	ice cream	sky

Use each pair to write a rhyming couplet to describe each picture.

32 OTM-1875 • SSR1-75 Poetry Prompts

Writing a Triplet

A triplet is three lines that rhyme. Each line has the same number of syllables.

Example:

> Look at the moon tonight,
> A round, white, shining light,
> It is a pretty sight!

Choose a group of rhyming words from the box.
Write a triplet on the lines provided.
Try to create as many as you can.

Rhyming Groups

sand	money	pine	pole	tree
band	honey	mine	mole	see
grand	bunny	valentine	hole	bee
sky	kite	pears	sweet	pie
by	sight	bears	eat	spy
fly	white	chairs	treat	cry

My Rhyming Triplets

1. _____

   _____

   _____

2. _____

   _____

   _____

3. _____

   _____

   _____

Section 5

Writing a Quatrain

A quatrain is a poem written in four lines --rhymed or unrhymed. Quatrains are frequently used in verse writing. They may be simple or complex with a variety of rhyming patterns. Quatrains may be written about life events, silly thoughts, serious feelings and nature.

Rhyming quatrains follow a variety of rhyming patterns.

Examples: **AABB** – lines 1 and 2 rhyme; lines 3 and 4 rhyme

There was once a rabbit with silver fur;	A
Her little neighbors look up to her,	A
Till she thought with pride in the moon-lit wood,	B
"The reason I'm white is because I'm good.	B

ABAB – lines 1 and 3 rhyme; lines 2 and 4 rhyme

He was a rat, and she was a rat,	A
And down in one hole they did dwell,	B
And both were as black as a witch's cat,	A
And they loved one another well.	B

ABCB – lines 2 and 4 rhyme; lines 1 and 3 do not rhyme

If all the world were apple-pie	A
And all the sea were ink,	B
And all the trees were bread and cheese	C
What would we have to drink?	B

AAAA – All four lines rhyme

Starlight, star bright	A
First star I see tonight	A
I wish I may, I wish I might	A
Have the wish I wish tonight.	A

Writing a Quatrain

Have your students search through poetry books in the library for quatrains. Each student could choose his/her favorite one and share it with the class. Each poem could be neatly recorded and illustrated and stored in class poetry book.

After you have read and shared quatrains with your class, record three or four on the chalkboard, chart paper or on an overhead. Have the students examine the rhyming pattern of each one. Once they have done this, have the students search for quatrains that match the rhyming patterns. They can be read and enjoyed by the entire class.

Next, practice writing quatrains with the entire class. When you think your students have had enough large group practice organize them into small groups. Provide each group with the same starting line and allow the students plenty of time to create their quatrains. Once completed each group will chorally read their quatrain. Discuss the quatrains and after positive comments, compile the quatrains into a class book.

The Dandelion

I saw him peeping from my lawn,
A tiny spot of yellow;
His face was one great big smile –
The jolly little fellow

The Poppy

High on a bright and sunny bed
A scarlet poppy grew;
And up it held its staring head
And thrust it full in view.

Section 5

Writing a Quatrain

A quatrain is a poem written in four lines. The lines may rhyme or be unrhymed. Quatrains that rhyme have a variety of rhyming patterns. Try writing your own quatrain, using the following directions.

1. Write your own first line of your quatrain or choose one from the list of first lines below.

• This morning as I walked to school   • I like sports of every kind

<table>
<tr><td>• This morning as I walked to school</td><td>• I like sports of every kind</td></tr>
<tr><td>• He tossed the pizza up so high</td><td>• Sometimes when I feel sad and blue</td></tr>
<tr><td>• The fluffy snowflakes gently fell</td><td>• If I was a bird with a snug little nest</td></tr>
<tr><td>• The raindrops pattered on the window pane</td><td>• A friend is someone who</td></tr>
<tr><td>• On our street lived a funny, old man</td><td>• Rock music is great to hear</td></tr>
<tr><td>• On the day that our dog died</td><td>• Birthday parties are great affairs</td></tr>
<tr><td>• Jeans are pants that are great to wear</td><td></td></tr>
</table>

2. Write your first line below. Quatrains can rhyme in a variety of ways such as: aaaa, abab, aabb, abcd. Now write the last three lines.

_____
(title)

_____

_____

_____

_____

_____

_____

3. Give your quatrain a title.

OTM-1875 • SSR1-75 Poetry Prompts

Section 5

Cinquain

Traditional cinquain is an unrhymed form of poetry consisting of five lines. A cinquain follows a specific pattern containing 22 syllables.

Line 1 – two syllable word or words announcing topic
Line 2 – four syllables describing the topic
Line 3 – six syllables expressing action
Line 4 – eight syllables expressing feeling
Line 5 – two syllable ending, synonym for topic

Cinquains do not have titles. The first line announces the topic.

Here are some cinquains to share with your class. Record them on the chalkboard, chart paper or an overhead and discuss the rhythm and form.

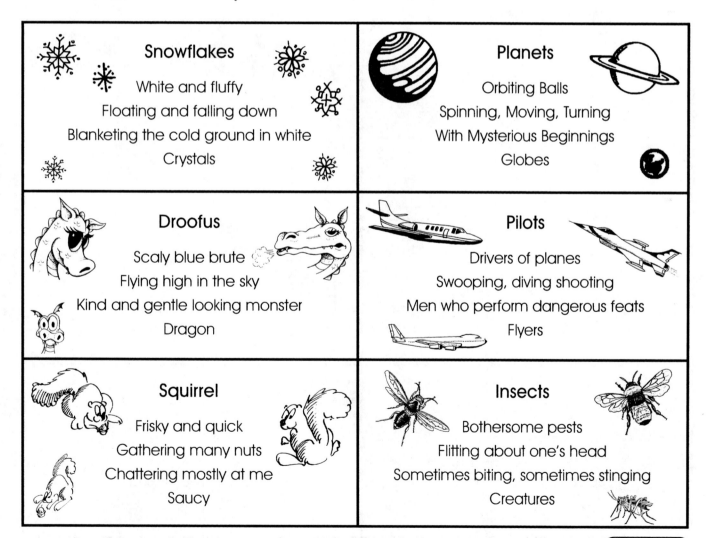

Snowflakes
White and fluffy
Floating and falling down
Blanketing the cold ground in white
Crystals

Planets
Orbiting Balls
Spinning, Moving, Turning
With Mysterious Beginnings
Globes

Droofus
Scaly blue brute
Flying high in the sky
Kind and gentle looking monster
Dragon

Pilots
Drivers of planes
Swooping, diving shooting
Men who perform dangerous feats
Flyers

Squirrel
Frisky and quick
Gathering many nuts
Chattering mostly at me
Saucy

Insects
Bothersome pests
Flitting about one's head
Sometimes biting, sometimes stinging
Creatures

Section 6

Cinquain

The traditional cinquain may be too difficult for some student to write. Another popular form used by teachers consists of the following steps.

one word topic *(noun)*
two describing words *(adjectives)*
three action words *(verbs)*
a four word phrase
a synonym for the topic

Cinquains do not have titles. The first line announces the topic.

Here are some cinquains that follow this pattern to share with your class. Record them on the chalkboard, chart paper, or an overhead. Read and discuss the rhythm and form.

Weeds

Nasty, bothersome
Growing, choking, destroying
Seen in every garden
Pests

Guinea

Fat, furry
Nibbling, munching, twitching
Funny little fur ball
Pet

Robins

Spring warblers
Flying, swooping, singing
Like to build nests
Birds

Warriors

Brutal cruel
Fighting, killing, looting
Silently sailing up rivers
Vikings

Lion

Scary, large
Leaps, pounces, springs
Surprises his prey easily
Beast

Apple

Red, glossy
Crunches, snaps, bruises
Makes a healthy snack
Fruit

Section 6

Writing a Cinquain

A cinquain is a five line poem written in a very special way. It is a form of free verse.

The steps below will help you write your own cinquain. Carefully read and follow each one.

1. Name a topic._____

2. Brainstorm for words that describe the topic.

    _____   _____   _____
    _____   _____   _____
    _____   _____   _____

3. Think of action words that describe the topic.

    _____   _____   _____
    _____   _____   _____
    _____   _____   _____

4. Think of some four-word phrases that describe the feeling in your topic.

    _____
    _____
    _____
    _____
    _____

5. Think of a synonym or word that refers to your topic. How many synonyms can you think of?

    _____   _____   _____
    _____   _____   _____
    _____   _____   _____

Circle the words and phrases that you liked the best from each step.

Section 6

Copy the circled words and phrases on the shape provided. Illustrate a picture of your cinquain in the box.

My Cinquain

_____

_____   _____

_____   _____   _____

_____

_____

by _____

Acrostic Poetry

An acrostic poem does not rhyme. The title or topic word is written, vertically down the page. Each word or phrase of the poem begins with a letter in the topic word or title.

The model of an acrostic poem looks like this:

Hats

H _____

A _____

T _____

S _____

Record samples of acrostic poems on the chalkboard, on chart paper or on an overhead for your students to see and read. Make sure that the letter of the first word in each line stands out by using a different colored marker, piece of chalk or overhead pen. Read the poems with your class. Discuss the pattern.

Sample Acrostic Poetry

Loveable	Determined	Eager	Reasonable
Interesting	Exciting	Devoted	Understanding
Smart	Active	Dedicated	Thoughtful
Attractive	Neat	Industrious	Honest
		Entertaining	

Sample Acrostic Poetry

Cranberries
Ham
Raisins
Icing
Sugar Cookies
Turkey
Mincemeat
Apples
Sausages

Tall and stately
Round you we gather
Excitedly waiting
Eager to see you glow.

Tortilla made of corn
Always so tasty
Containing delicious meat
Often fried on a griddle

Scattered everywhere
Even in sidewalk cracks
Eventually become plants
Downy and fluffy
Small and brown

Beautiful butterflies
Ugly beetles
Gigantic moths
Stinging bees

March is a blustery month
Always cold and windy
Rattling windows and shaking doors
Calling plants and animals to awaken
Hurriedly chasing winter away.

Lovely leaves
Excite the world
Autumn is your time
For you to show your beauty

Terrible tigers
In jungles green
Growl and roar,
Everywhere they've been
Racing after animals

Carefree and playful Cupid
Using his magic bow
Putting arrows of love
Into young lovers
Down on the earth below.

Dashing through the forests
Expert, graceful, jumpers
Eating twigs and leaves
Resting in a safe glen.

Crocus is a spring flower
Rising above the snow
Only blooms in the springtime
Cuplike flower
Usually white, purple or yellow
Small and pretty

Wars are deadly
Armies fighting fiercely
Ruining cities and towns
Soldiers dying in the battlefields

Stately and powerful
Protector of the pyramids
Head like a man and body of a lion
In the hot, dry desert
Noble statues
X-citing to see

Section 7

Acrostic Poetry

Acrostic poetry appears easy to write but does require careful thinking and planning in order to create a meaningful writing. Begin with three or four letter words in order to give your students a positive writing experience.

Practice writing acrostic poems on the chalkboard with your class. Encourage your students to use a dictionary or thesaurus to hunt for words. Follow the steps below.

Step 1: Chose a three or four letter word.

BATS

Step 2: Brainstorm and list words or word phrases that describe or relate to the topic. On the chalkboard create a similar chart. Record your student responses on it.

B	A	T	S
Brown fur	Awful looking	Travel at night	Seek insects
Busy at night	Always fly	Timid creatures	Sleep in caves
Black and Furry	Animals	Toes with claws	Small mammals
Big, broad wings	Attics are homes	Tastes fruit	Sleep during the day
	After insects		Small, sharp teeth
	Amazing animals		

Step 3: Write the word vertically on the chalkboard.

B _____

A _____

T _____

S _____

Acrostic Poetry

Step 4: As a class select the words or word phrases for each letter. Circle the ones that you will be using. Write the appropriate one beside each letter. Use the rest of the words or word phrases to make other acrostic poems about bats.

Black and furry
After insects
Travel at night
Sleep during the day

Big, broad wings
Always fly
Timid creatures
Sleep in caves

Brown fur
Awful looking
Toes with claws
Small, sharp teeth

Step 5: Have your students select or vote for the acrostic poem that they like the best. Then they can copy it neatly and illustrate the poem.

Step 6: Once your students are comfortable writing three and four letter acrostics then introduce five to six letter words. Discuss small phrases of two to three words or more. Use a similar format following the steps mentioned on "Writing an Acrostic".

Writing an Acrostic Poem

Remember: An acrostic poem does not rhyme and its topic or title is written vertically down the page.

Follow each step below carefully and you will successfully write your own acrostic poem.

Step 1: From the box below choose a word that interests you. Circle the one that you chose.

rain	toes	feet	bear	love	grin
snow	nose	hair	lion	soap	nest
hail	lips	song	milk	hate	tree
boys	eyes	bird	rink	blue	weed
girls	hand	tart	cake	July	fish

Step 2: Write each letter of your chosen word on the line at the top of each section of the chart below. Brainstorm and list words and phrases that describe your word.

____	____	____	____

OTM-1875 • SSR1-75 POETRY PROMPTS

Section 7

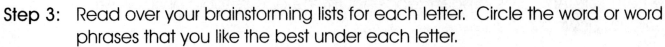

Writing an Acrostic Poem

Step 3: Read over your brainstorming lists for each letter. Circle the word or word phrases that you like the best under each letter.

Step 4: Write the letters of your word in each box provided vertically.

☐ _____

☐ _____

☐ _____

☐ _____

Step 5: Write the words and word phrases that you have circled on your brainstorming chart on the lines above beside the letters.

Step 6: Recopy your acrostic poem and illustrate it in the following box.

My Acrostic Poem

Limericks

A limerick is a humorous poem of five lines. It is arranged in the following pattern.

Line One .... a

Line Two .... a

Line Three........................ b

Line Four .... b

Line Five .... a

Here is a limerick written by Edward Lear.

> There was an Old Man with a beard,
>
> Who said, "It is just as I feared!
>
> Two owls and a hen,
>
> Four larks and a wren,
>
> Have all built their nests in my beard."

Edward Lear, a famous poet, made the limerick popular in the early years of the 19th century. Limericks are funny, witty and often silly. They have been used to criticize and make fun of politicians and famous people.

Limericks do have a definite rhythm pattern. Be sure to share plenty of limericks with students so they can feel the rhythm and hear the rhyming words.

Plan a Limerick Hunt in the resource center (Library) with your students. They are to look through poetry books to find limericks. The poems are to be recorded, memorized and acted out by the students. Limericks could also be collected and written in books for the classroom.

Limericks

Share any of the following limericks with your class so they may hear the rhythm and rhyming words. Record them on the chalkboard, chart paper or an overhead.

There once was a little girl named Lisa, Who loved eating pepperoni and cheese pizza. Every day she would munch, On pizza for lunch. Until through the door she couldn't squeez-a	There once was a sad car named Rusty. Who sat in a barn getting dusty. Once he was new, Over roads he flew Now he's dingy and smells very musty.
There once was a family of owls. For mice, father was always on the prowl, Mother brewed a mouse stew. The owlets said, "Whoo-whoo Tomorrow night can we have fowl?"	There once was a clown named Bobo. Who was always dressed like a hobo. He walked on a wire, While eating some fire. Then played a cool song on an oboe.
There once was a Daffodil named Dilly Who always acted very silly He would stand tall And try to call His friends with his trumpet so frilly	There once was a crocodile named Blooze Who spent most of his time having a snooze One day by surprise He was shot at sunrise And now your teacher is wearing him as shoes!
There once was a unicorn named Horace Who sang in the unicorn chorus. When he sang songs His horn grew so long That he couldn't walk through the forest.	There once was a llama named Mack, Who was carrying a big, heavy pack. How he grunted and groaned, My aching back he moaned! And plopped down on the mountain track.

Let's Work With Limericks

A limerick is a humorous poem. They are fun to read and write.

Remember:

1. A limerick has five lines.
2. Lines one, two and five rhyme.
3. Line five refers to line one.
4. Lines three and four rhyme.
5. Lines three and four are shorter.
6. There is a definite rhythm pattern.
7. A limerick usually starts with "There once was" or "There was".

Complete the following limericks with rhyming words.

There once was a little, old man named _____,
Who loved to eat foods that were _____.
He ate strawberries for _____,
And cherries by the _____.
Till he was so sick he went to _____.

There once was a prisoner named _____,
He escaped on a raft out to _____.
The waters got _____.
His journey was _____,
But alas, he was finally _____.

There once was a spider named _____,
Whose appearance looked terribly _____.
All the girl spiders would _____,
When Harry came _____.
That's why Harry would never _____.

There once was a moth named _____,
Who was afraid of the _____.
He clung to a tree _____,
Where no one could see _____,
And waited for the dark of the _____.

Section 8

Let's Write a Limerick

1. Choose one of the beginning lines that you like the best.

> There once was a witch named Tilly,
>
> There once was a bunny named Sunny,
>
> There was a man who lived in a shack,
>
> There once was a bullfrog named Matt,
>
> There once was a squid named Sid,
>
> There once was a creature named Jars,
>
> There once was a bug named Sam,
>
> There once was a beaver named Fred,
>
> There was an old lady in town,

2. Write your beginning line here.

    _____

3. Make a list of words that rhyme with the last word in your first line.

    _____   _____   _____

    _____   _____   _____

    _____   _____   _____

    _____   _____   _____

4. Think of a second line. It must rhyme with line one. Write it here.

    _____

5. Write two short sentences that describe the topic. Make sure they rhyme.

    _____

    _____

Section 8

6. Write the last line. It must rhyme with line one and two. Check your list of rhyming words.

_____

7. Once you have completed your limerick copy it on the lines below and illustrate it.

My Limerick

_____
_____
_____
_____
_____

Picture

Section 8

Writing a Limerick

Use these steps to help you write your own limerick.

Step 1: Choose the name of a person, place or thing that you want your limerick to be about. Write the name on the line.

_____

Step 2: Make up your first line using the word that you choose. Write it on the line.

_____

Step 3: Brainstorm for words that rhyme with the last word of sentence one. Record them on the lines provided.

_____   _____   _____

_____   _____   _____

_____   _____   _____

Step 4: Create your second line. Make sure it rhymes with line one. Write it on the line.

_____

Step 5: Think of two short sentences that rhyme. They must describe the topic. Write them on the line.

_____

_____

Step 6: Create your last line. It must rhyme with lines one and two.   Write it on the line.

_____

Step 7: Copy your limerick neatly on a sheet of paper and illustrate it.

Section 8

Haiku

Haiku poetry was first written by the Japanese. The haiku is a three-line, seventeen syllable, unrhymed poem, which usually describes nature. This form of poetry describes a moment of beauty that arouses feelings and thoughts.

There are some students, who for one reason or another, may not be able to handle the exact 17 syllables of traditional haiku, but are able to handle a simplified pattern.

Example:

Where it takes place	In the flower bed
What is taking place	the bee flits about the flowers
When it happens	on a summer's day

A traditional haiku consists of seventeen syllables organized into three lines.

Example:

Line One: 5 syllables	In the quaint garden
Line Two: 7 syllables	the lovely daffodils swayed
Line Three: 5 syllables	in the gentle breeze

Share the following haiku with your class. Record them on the chalkboard, chart paper or an overhead. Read and clap the rhythm of each one. Discuss the feeling it emits.

Sample Haiku

In a deep, dark hole
a ground hog stretches and stirs
in February

On a nest up high
Mother Robin sits so still
in the early spring.

Section 9

Sample Haiku

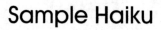

On a tall, oak tree the green leaves fluttered softly as the breeze passed through.	In the rainforest the hairy, green sloth is seen hanging upside down.
On the cold, hard ground snowflakes floated softly down one day in winter.	Above the stable the sparkling star shone brightly showing us the way.
On the tin rooftop raindrops hammered so loudly during a summer's day.	Growing in Flanders see the bright, blood-red poppies between the crosses.
In the dark, gray sky the lightning flashed so brightly lighting the dark night.	In a dark forest there stood a tall sequoia serenely quiet.
Out in the garden the fat snowman stood proudly in the warm bright sun.	In the hot desert the camel works very hard carrying big loads.
In the blue, clear sky fluffy clouds floated around while I was playing	In the jungle deep colorful lovebirds sit high lovingly cooing.
Beside the pond's edge stood a silent doe drinking at the dusk of day.	On the river's ice the skaters glide quickly one cold winter's day.

Writing a 'Where, What, When' Haiku

Follow the steps below.

Step 1: Look at the picture of the butterfly.

Think about butterflies.
Where do you see them?
What are they like?
When do you see them?

Step 2: Brainstorm and write a list of phrases that describe where the butterfly may be

_____   _____   _____

_____   _____   _____

_____   _____   _____

Step 3: Brainstorm and write a list of phrases that describe what is happening.

_____   _____   _____

_____   _____   _____

_____   _____   _____

Step 4: Brainstorm and write a list of phrases that tell when it happened.

_____   _____   _____

_____   _____   _____

_____   _____   _____

Step 5: Choose a phrase from each of your lists to complete a main idea or thought. Write your phrases below. Illustrate your haiku.

_____

_____

_____

_____

Section 9

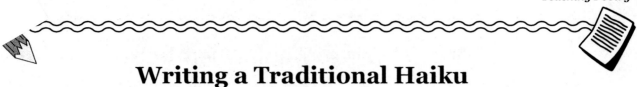

Writing a Traditional Haiku

Before students attempt writing a traditional haiku provide several practice sessions with them.

Focus on the following:

1. nature
2. help students brainstorm colorful phrases
3. assist them with the syllabication of each phrase
4. practice writing several haiku

Follow these steps:

Step 1: Display a seasonal picture on the chalkboard.
Discuss the scene with your students.
Question them on: where the picture takes place
the objects in the scene
the action taking place
when it is happening
its mood and feelings

Step 2: Brainstorm for phrases that describe the scene. List them on the chalkboard. Do not worry about syllabication at this point.

Step 3: Review the syllables for syllabication. If there are too many syllables or too few change the phrases immediately so that you have only 5 syllable and 7 syllable phrases.

Step 4: When all the phrases have the required number of syllables, ask a student to choose a 5 syllable phrase to begin the haiku. Explain to the students they are painting a word picture.

Writing a Traditional Haiku

Step 5:   Read the phrase to the class. Have them think about it and choose a phrase that has 7 syllables that preserves the meaning and tone. Write it as the second line of the haiku.

Step 6:   Finish the poem with the selection of a 5 syllable phrase for the third line.

Step 7:   Write several more poems with the phrases.

Step 8:   Read the poems with your class. Have your students vote to see which haiku they liked the best.

Step 9:   Each student will choose a haiku, copy it neatly and illustrate it.

Step 10: Repeat this process several times before the students independently write a haiku.

On a quiet street

sits my small, white, cosy house

filled with peace and love.

Writing a Traditional Haiku

Choose one of the following topics or think of one of your own.

winter	ocean	birds	bears	moon
spring	leaves	seashore	apples	stars
summer	trees	meadow	snow	clouds
autumn	whales	mountains	rain	water

My topic is _____

Step 1: Think about the topic that you chose. Write words or phrases that describe your feelings about it. Write ten colorful phrases below.

_____

_____

_____

_____

_____

_____

_____

_____

_____

_____

Step 2: Check each phrase to see if it is either 5 syllables or 7 syllables long. Change the ones that are too long or too short.

Step 3: Select a 5 syllable phrase which makes the best starter. Write it on the line.

_____

Step 4: Select a 7 syllable phrase that keeps the meaning of the mood of the first line. Write it on the line

_____

Step 5: For the third line, select a 5 syllable phrase from your list, which will end your haiku. Write it on the line.

_____

Step 6: Record lines one, two and three of your haiku on the lines below. Proofread your poem and edit it for spelling errors and the required number of syllables.

_____

_____

_____

Step Seven: Rewrite your haiku neatly on the lines in the frame and illustrate it.

Alphabet Poetry

Alphabet poetry is referred to as inventive poetry. They do not always make good sense but they are fun and challenging to write. The complete alphabet or parts of it may be used to write a poem.

Example:

Apples, beautiful, crisp,   A

delicious, edible, fruit,   Big

good to eat, hang from trees   Careless

in the orchard, just for us,   Dog

munchy, nice to eat,   Eats

Often in pies, packed in lunches,   Frozen

Quick snacks, ripe, sweet,   Green

Useful, various colors,   Hamburger

wonderful food, x-tremely good,

Yummy, z-apples

While writing an alphabet poem the writer must focus on the topic and arranges the words or word phrases in alphabetical order.

Read other alphabet poems to your class so they will become more acquainted with the style and form of alphabet poetry.

Then work with your class following the steps below.

Step 1:   Select a topic and discuss it thoroughly.

Step 2:   List the letters of the alphabet on the chalkboard. Brainstorm for words pertaining to the topic. Record each word or word phrase beside the correct letter of the alphabet.

Step 3:   Try to group the words to make short phrases, or make phrases by adding words.

Step 4:   Have the students edit and refine the words and phrases in the poem.

Step 5:   The students will copy the finished product neatly and illustrate it.

Step 6:   Practice this verse form several times before the students work on one independently.

Section 10

Alphabet Poetry

An alphabet poem uses the letters of the alphabet. You may use the entire alphabet or part of it.

Choose a topic or pick one of your own.

Traveling	Shoes	Food	Animals	Countries
Baseball	Hats	Toys	Vehicles	Books
Hockey	Clothes	Names	Music	Candy

Brainstorm words that describe the topic. Use your dictionary to help you. Edit your poem for spelling and make the necessary changes.

Topic: _____

A _____   J _____   S _____
    _____   _____   _____
B _____   K _____   T _____
    _____   _____   _____
C _____   L _____   U _____
    _____   _____   _____
D _____   M _____   V _____
    _____   _____   _____
E _____   N _____   W _____
    _____   _____   _____
F _____   O _____   X _____
    _____   _____   _____
G _____   P _____   Y _____
    _____   _____   _____
H _____   Q _____   Z _____
    _____   _____   _____
I _____   R _____
    _____   _____

Alphabet Poetry

Write your poem on the lines.

A X O Z B C T F G T H S U

L

N

Q

B

D

G

I

K

J

_____
(Topic)

A	_____	N	_____
B	_____	O	_____
C	_____	P	_____
D	_____	Q	_____
E	_____	K	_____
F	_____	S	_____
G	_____	T	_____
H	_____	U	_____
I	_____	V	_____
J	_____	W	_____
K	_____	X	_____
L	_____	Y	_____
M	_____	Z	_____

H

I

P

J

A

B

N

C

L

M K R T W V O P F D S T Y

Section 10

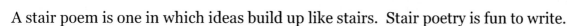

Stair Poetry

A stair poem is one in which ideas build up like stairs. Stair poetry is fun to write.

Step 1: Write the topic of the poem.

Step 2: Write three adjectives that describe the topic.

Step 3: Write the name of the place or time of the topic.

Step 4: Write a summary of the topic.

Example:

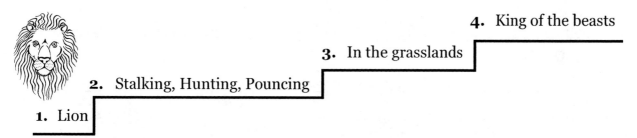

4. King of the beasts

3. In the grasslands

2. Stalking, Hunting, Pouncing

1. Lion

Share these samples with your class.

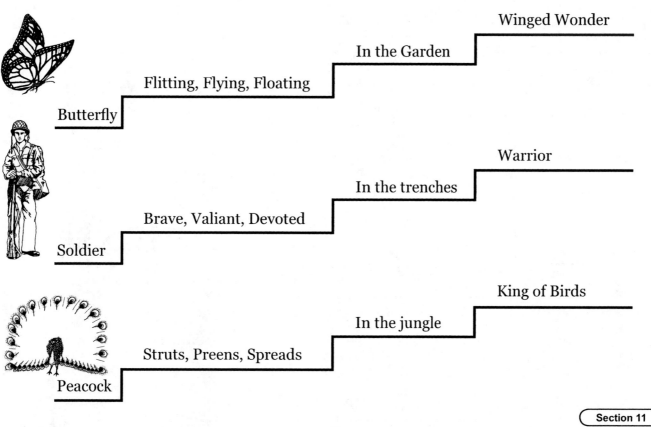

Winged Wonder

In the Garden

Flitting, Flying, Floating

Butterfly

Warrior

In the trenches

Brave, Valiant, Devoted

Soldier

King of Birds

In the jungle

Struts, Preens, Spreads

Peacock

Section 11

Stair Poetry

A stair poem is one in which ideas build up like stairs.

Step 1: Write the topic of your stair poem on the line.

_____

Step 2: Write adjectives that describe your topic on the lines.

_____   _____   _____

_____   _____   _____

Step 3: Write the name of the place or the time in a phrase. Think of three. Write
them on the lines below.

_____

_____

_____

_____

Step 4: Write another name for the topic.

_____   _____   _____

Step 5: Choose the adjectives and phrase you like the best. Write your stair
poem on the steps below. Illustrate it.

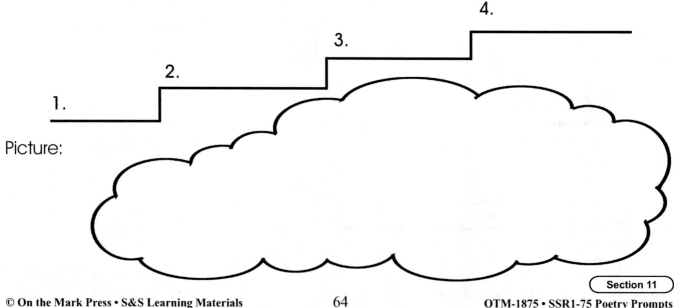

Picture:

Section 11

Diamante

The diamante is another form of unrhymed poetry similar to the cinquain. Its physical shape on paper is in the shape of a diamond. Diamante is the Italian word for diamond, hence its name. The same teaching strategies used to teach the cinquain can be applied while teaching the writing of the diamante. There are two types of diamante. One uses synonyms while the other uses antonyms for the topic.

Form 1: Using Synonyms

Line One:	Topic *(noun)*
Line Two:	Two describing words *(adjectives)*
Line Three:	Three action words *(verbs or "ing" action words)*
Line Four:	A four word phrase expressing feeling about the topic
Line Five:	Three action words *(verbs or "ing" words)*
Line Six:	Two describing words *(adjectives)*
Line Seven:	Ending word *(noun)*, synonym, strong emotional word for the topic

Examples:

Children
Playful, happy
Running, jumping, hopping
Bringing joy and happiness
Giving, loving, sharing
Active, noisy
Youngsters

Apples
Crispy, crunchy
Growing, hanging, ripening
Filled with healthy vitamins
Falling, rolling, rotting
Sweet, delicious
Fruit

Section 12

Synonym Diamante

A synonym diamante begins and ends with a pair of synonyms. Synonyms are words that have similar meanings.

Follow the steps below carefully to write your own synonym diamante.

Step 1: Lines 1 and 7

Choose a pair of synonyms. Record them on the line below.

_____

One synonym will be for line 1 of your poem and the other one will be for line 7. Record them on the appropriate lines.

Step 2: Line 2

Brainstorm for adjectives that describe the topic.

_____ _____ _____
_____ _____ _____
_____ _____ _____
_____ _____ _____

Step 3: Line 3

Think of verbs that end in "**ing**" or "**ed**" that describe the topic.

_____ _____ _____
_____ _____ _____
_____ _____ _____
_____ _____ _____

Step 4: Line 4

Write four word phrases which express feeling about the topic.

_____
_____
_____
_____

Section 12

Step 5: Line 5

Think of action words that could be used with the topic. They must end with "**ed**" or "**ing**".

_____	_____	_____
_____	_____	_____
_____	_____	_____
_____	_____	_____

Step 6: Line 6

Think of more adjectives that describe the topic.

_____	_____	_____
_____	_____	_____
_____	_____	_____
_____	_____	_____

From your previous brainstorming choose words to create your own synonym diamante.

1. Topic Word   _____

2. Two adjectives   _____

3. Three action words   _____

4. One phrase   _____

5. Three action words   _____

6. Two adjectives   _____

7. Synonym   _____

Step 7:

Copy your diamante neatly and illustrate it.

Section 12

An Antonym Diamante

An antonym diamante begins and ends with words that are opposite in meaning.

Example:

Kind

Warm, good

Caring, giving, sharing

Mother, Father, strangers, enemies

Terrifying, hurting, frightening

Mean, unkind

Cruel

In this form of diamante we must work from both ends.

Use the following steps while working with your students.

Step 1: Name the topic noun *(Line 1)*

Step 2: Decide on the antonym *(Line 7)*

Step 3: Choose two describing words for the topic noun.

Step 4: Choose two describing words for the antonym.

Step 5: Think of three action words for the topic noun.

Step 6: Think of three action words for the antonym.

Step 7: Decide on four nouns. Two for the topic noun and two for the antonym or ending word.

Example:

Line One	Mother
Line Two	Caring, loving
Line Three	Embracing, hugging, laughing
Line Four	Female, Wife, Male, Husband
Line Five	Working, providing, sharing
Line Six	Kind, Warm
Line Seven	Father

Section 12

Antonym Diamante

An antonym diamante begins and ends with a pair of antonyms. Antonyms are words that are opposite in meaning.

Follow the steps below to write your own antonym diamante.

In this form of diamante we must work from both ends.

Step 1: Writing Lines 1 and 7

Think of pairs of opposites. Write them on the lines provided.

_____   _____   _____

_____   _____   _____

Circle the pair of antonyms you liked the best. Record them on the first and last line of the poetry form.

Step 2: Writing Line 2

Think of words that describe the noun in Line 1. Write them on the lines provided.

_____   _____   _____

_____   _____   _____

_____   _____   _____

Circle the adjectives that you liked the best. Write the adjectives on line 2 of the poetry form.

Step 3: Writing Line 3

Think of verbs that relate to the noun in line 1. The words should end with "**ed**" or "**ing**".

_____   _____   _____

_____   _____   _____

_____   _____   _____

Circle the verbs that you liked the best. Write the verbs on line 3 of the poetry form.

Section 12

Step 4: Writing Line 4

Think of the two nouns that relate to the antonym on line 1 and two nouns that relate to the antonym on line 7.

Antonym on Line 1   _____   _____

Antonym on Line 7   _____   _____

Record these four words on line 4 of your poem.

Step 5: Writing Line 5

Think of three verbs that relate to the antonym in line 7. Each word must end with "ed" or "ing'.

_____   _____   _____

_____   _____   _____

_____   _____   _____

Circle the verbs that you liked the best. Write the words on line 5 of the poetry form.

Step 6: Writing Line 6

Think of two words that describe the antonym on line 7

Circle the adjectives that you liked the best. Record them on line 6 of the poetry form.

Line One   _____
Line Two   _____
Line Three   _____
Line Four   _____
Line Five   _____
Line Six   _____
Line Seven   _____

Step 7:

Copy neatly and illustrate your diamante on another sheet of paper.

Section 12

Clerihew Poetry

The clerihew is a form of poetry created by Edmund Clerihew Bently. It consists of four lines of two rhyming couplets. The clerihew's rhyming pattern is AABB. The poem usually describes a person in a humorous way. The first line contains the person's name. Quite often the clerihew is written about a famous person. Sometimes the name is reversed for rhyming purposes.

> **Example:**   Jonathan Brown
> or
> Brown, Jonathan

Have your students participate in the following steps.

Step 1:   Select the name of a famous person or a well known story character. Record names on the chalkboard and select one.

Step 2:   Decide which way the name will be written. This will depend on the name word that lends itself best to rhyming.

Step 3:   Brainstorm for words that rhyme with the name part chosen. List the words on the chalkboard.

> **Example:** down, town, clown, frown, crown

Using the list brainstormed, guide your students to creating a second line.

> **Example:** Jonathan Brown
> Was a funny fat clown.

Step 4:   Brainstorm with your class for possible third lines. Record them on the chalkboard. Have the students select the one that goes best with the first two lines. Record it with lines one and two.

> **Example:** Jonathan Brown
> Was a funny, fat clown.
> He rode in a little car

Step 5:   Brainstorm for words that rhyme with the last word in line three.

> **Example:** bar, far, jar, tar, star, spar, scar, mar, char

Step 6:   With your students brainstorm for the fourth line of the poem using one of the rhyming words in the list. Record line four with the other lines.

> **Example:** Jonathan Brown
> Was a funny, fat clown.
> He rode in a little car
> But he never traveled very far.

Step 7:   Practice writing clerihew poetry with your students using this format several times before they do one independently or with a partner.

Writing a Clerihew Poem

Remember: A clerihew poem consists of two rhyming couplets that tell something about a person.

Follow the steps below to help create your own clerihew poem.

Step 1: Write the name of a person on the line.

_____

Step 2: Brainstorm for words that rhyme with the name.

_____

Step 3: Create your second line. Write it on the line.

_____

Step 4: Think of a line that will go well with lines one and two. Record it on the line.

_____

Step 5: Think of words that rhyme with the last word of line three. Record them on the line.

_____

Step 6: Create line four using the rhyming word that you chose. Record line four on the line.

_____

Step 7: Copy the four lines of your clerihew on the lines provided. Share it with a classmate.

_____

_____

_____

_____

Section 13

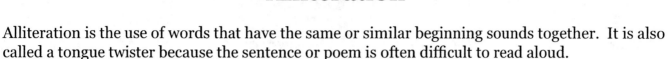

Alliteration

Alliteration is the use of words that have the same or similar beginning sounds together. It is also called a tongue twister because the sentence or poem is often difficult to read aloud.

Examples:

> Simple Simon saw Silly Sally sitting on the shaggy sofa.
>
> Peter Piper picked a peck of pickled peppers.
>
> Big blue balls bounced beautifully on the back of the buffalo.
>
> Wee Willie Winkle whistled wonderfully well while he walked.
>
> How much wood would a woodchuck chuck if a woodchuck could chuck wood?

Teach your students alliteration using names.

Follow the steps below.

Step 1: Record a name on the chalkboard that is not recognized in the class. Example: Ruth

Step 2: Have your class brainstorm for words that begin the same way. List the words on the chalkboard.

Step 3: The students will build and expand the word into a sentence using the list of brainstormed words.

> **Example:**
>
> Ruth
> Ruth runs regularly.
> Rugged Ruth runs regularly.
> Rugged Ruth runs regularly in red.
> Rugged Ruth runs regularly in red to Richmond.

Step 4: Repeat the steps several times for practice.

Step 5: When the students are ready, divide them into groups of two or three or four to write name alliterations. They could use their first or middle names. Encourage the use of a dictionary.

Section 14

Alliteration or Tongue Twister Poetry

Alliteration or Tongue Twister is a silly sentence in which all or most of the words begin with the same sound. The sentence should be as long as you can make it. This technique adds interest to your writing.

Write your own alliteration sentence or Tongue Twister.

Step 1: Choose a beginning sound. On the lines below, list as many words as you can that begin with the sound.

_____   _____   _____

_____   _____   _____

_____   _____   _____

_____   _____   _____

Step 2: Use the words to write alliteration sentences or tongue twisters. Write as many sentences as you can.

_____

_____

_____

_____

_____

_____

Step 3: Copy and illustrate the best one here.

My Alliteration Sentence or Tongue Twister

by _____

_____

_____

_____

_____

Metaphors

A metaphor is a word, phrase, or sentence, which compares one thing to another without using like, as, than, similar to, or resembles.

Examples:

> Barry is a walking computer.
>
> Mrs. Fitchet's bark is worse that her bite.
>
> His heart is an iceberg.
>
> The army of ants attacked the fallen ice cream cone on the sidewalk.

Match the sentence parts to write good metaphors. Write the correct sentence part on each line, from the box under the sentences.

1. My boss is _____ .

2. This is a monster _____ .

3. Her eyes were _____ .

4. The dress is a _____ .

5. The cloud is a _____ .

6. The tall tree is a _____ .

7. The eagle is a _____ .

8. Green grass is _____ .

9. He is a snail when _____ .

10. Her heart is _____ .

soaring winged creature	of a problem
colorful rainbow	soldier guarding the gate
puffy, white cottonball	diamonds in the sunlight
he works at school	the forest's carpet
a bear	a fountain of kindness

Similies

A simile is a word, phrase, or sentence that compares two things using the words like, as, similar to, or resembles to highlight the comparison.

Examples:

as fat as a pig	felt like two cents
as light as a feather	eyes like stars
as cold as ice	waddled like a duck
as strong as steel	worked like a horse

Use a simile from the box below to complete each sentence.

1. Her baby sister is _____ .

2. He sanded the table until it felt _____ .

3. The boys were _____ .

4. The little girl's eyes _____ .

5. It had not rained for months and the land was _____ .

6. The mouse disappeared into the wall _____ when he saw the cat.

7. When Bobby came in from the cold he had _____ .

8. The giant roared with a voice _____ .

9. The water on the lake was _____ .

10. For days the man had not eaten and he was _____ .

as thin as a rail	cheeks like roses
as loud as thunder	dry as a bone
sparkled like diamonds	as smooth as silk
as busy as bees	as cute as a button
as smooth as glass	as quick as a wink

Section 14

Similes and Metaphors

Using similies and metaphors will make your writing more creative and interesting. Remember a simile is a comparison of two things using the words like or as. A metaphor is a comparison of two things without the use of like or as.

Complete each simile and metaphor in an interesting way.

Similes

1. The dog ate _____ .
2. The sun was _____ .
3. The wet cat looked _____ .
4. The ice was _____ .
5. The stars sparkled _____ .
6. That big rock is _____ .
7. The round moon was _____ .
8. The hole in the ground was _____ .
9. Her face was _____ .
10. The wolf was _____ .

Metaphors

1. The mountain of laundry _____ .
2. Her smooth skin was _____ .
3. The fluffy cloud was _____ .
4. The rock is _____ .
5. Snow is _____ .
6. A stream is _____ .
7. The angry bear _____ .
8. The wind blew _____ .
9. The rain fell _____ .
10. The tree stood _____ .

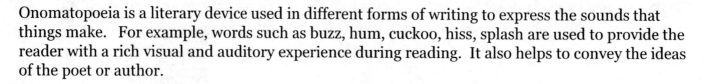

Onomatopaeia

Onomatopoeia is a literary device used in different forms of writing to express the sounds that things make. For example, words such as buzz, hum, cuckoo, hiss, splash are used to provide the reader with a rich visual and auditory experience during reading. It also helps to convey the ideas of the poet or author.

Examples:

> The boy slurped his soup
>
> The car came to a screeching stop.
>
> The cows stood in the field mooing.
>
> The wind howled around the house.

Have your students browse through pieces of literature to locate various ways the writers used anomatopoeia in their writings.

List the devices they find on a chart or have them read aloud.

Provide your students with a whole-class experience identifying onomatopoeia words that characterize the phrases below. Record them on a chart or the chalkboard. The students will brainstorm for words that give sound to the phrases.

1. the ceiling falling down
2. water dripping
3. a rooster
4. eating potato chips
5. car horns
6. pig snorting
7. creaking of a door
8. walking in a puddle
9. cracking a whip
10. walking on peanut shells
11. a horse walking
12. a chicken
13. an angry dog
14. a train starting up

Working With Onomatopoeia

Onomatopoeia is a literary term used by writers for words that sound like what they mean. Everyone knows the animal that is represented by "cluck cluck" or the message relayed by the word "bang".

Beside each phrase , record the word or words from the box below that would represent a better picture in your mind.

1. a cow lowing _____

2. a bell ringing _____

3. water going down the drain _____

4. a tap dripping _____

5. a donkey braying _____

6. a train starting up _____

7. a grandfather clock _____

8. walking on crusty snow _____

9. a balloon breaking _____

10. a lamb bleating _____

11. the wind blowing _____

12. a wolf calling _____

13. hail hitting a metal roof _____

14. a tugboat's horn _____

crunch, crunch	chug, chug, chug	gurgle
howling	hee-haw	moo
toot, toot	moaning	rat-a-tat-tat
bang	baa, baa	ding dong
tick, tock	ping, ping	

Section 14

Using Onomatopaeia

Onomatopoeia is a literary term used by writers to make their writings more interesting for their readers.

Example:

Which sentence below makes a better mental picture? Put a check mark in the box.

☐ Raindrops hit the glass of my window.

☐ Raindrops pitter-patter on the glass of my window.

Try rewriting each sentence below using onomatapoeia.

1. The big balloon exploded!

   _____

2. The wood in the fireplace was burning.

   _____

3. The silly, little witch was laughing.

   _____

4. Father hit the table with his hand and shouted loudly.

   _____

5. The steam coming out of the pipe made noise.

   _____

6. The boy ate his soup loudly and quickly.

   _____

7. The truck came to a sudden stop.

   _____

8. The water went down the bathtub drain.

   _____

9. The race car sped off.

   _____

10. The wind blew through the evergreen trees.

    _____

Section 14

Publication Listing

Publication Listing

Code #	Title and Grade
SSN1-100	Indian in the Cupboard NS Gr. 4-6
SSPC-05	Insects B/W Pictures
SSPC-10	Inuit B/W Pictures
SSJ1-10	Inuit Community Gr. 3-4
SSN1-85	Ira Sleeps Over NS Gr. 1-3
SSN1-93	Iron Man NS Gr. 4-6
SSN1-193	Island of the Blue Dolphins NS 4-6
SSB1-11	It's a Dogs World Gr. 2-3
SSM1-05	It's a Marshmallow World Gr. 3
SSK1-05	It's About Time Gr. 2-4
SSC1-41	It's Christmas Time Gr. 3
SSH1-04	It's Circus Time Gr. 1
SSC1-43	It's Groundhog Day Gr. 3
SSB1-75	It's Maple Syrup Time Gr. 2-4
SSC1-40	It's Trick or Treat Time Gr. 2
SSN1-65	James & The Giant Peach NS 4-6
SSN1-106	Jane Eyre NS Gr. 7-8
SSPC-25	Japan B/W Pictures
SSA1-06	Japan Gr. 5-8
SSC1-05	Joy of Christmas Gr. 2
SSN1-161	Julie of the Wolves NS Gr. 7-8
SSB1-81	Jungles Gr. 2-3
SSE1-02	Junior Music for Fall Gr. 4-6
SSE1-05	Junior Music for Spring Gr. 4-6
SSE1-06	Junior Music for Winter Gr. 4-6
SSN1-151	Kate NS Gr. 4-6
SSN1-95	Kidnapped in the Yukon NS Gr. 4-6
SSN1-140	Kids at Bailey School Gr. 2-4
SSN1-176	King of the Wind NS Gr. 4-6
SSF1-29	Klondike Gold Rush Gr. 4-6
SSF1-33	Labour Movement in Canada Gr. 7-8
SSN1-152	Lamplighter NS Gr. 4-6
SSB1-98	Learning About Dinosaurs Gr. 3
SSN1-38	Learning About Giants Gr. 4-6
SSK1-22	Learning About Measurement Gr. 1-3
SSB1-46	Learning About Mice Gr. 3-5
SSK1-09	Learning About Money CDN Gr. 1-3
SSK1-19	Learning About Money USA Gr. 1-3
SSK1-23	Learning About Numbers Gr. 1-3
SSB1-69	Learning About Rocks & Soils Gr. 2-3
SSK1-08	Learning About Shapes Gr. 1-3
SSB1-100	Learning About Simple Machines 1-3
SSK1-04	Learning About the Calendar Gr. 2-3
SSK1-10	Learning About Time Gr. 1-3
SSH1-17	Learning About Transportation Gr. 1
SSB1-02	Leaves Gr. 2-3
SSN1-50	Legends Gr. 4-6
SSC1-27	Lest We Forget Gr. 4-6
SSJ1-13	Let's Look at Canada Gr. 4-6
SSJ1-16	Let's Visit Alberta Gr. 2-4
SSJ1-15	Let's Visit British Columbia Gr. 2-4
SSJ1-03	Let's Visit Canada Gr. 3
SSJ1-18	Let's Visit Manitoba Gr. 2-4
SSJ1-21	Let's Visit New Brunswick Gr. 2-4
SSJ1-27	Let's Visit NFLD & Labrador Gr. 2-4
SSJ1-30	Let's Visit North West Terr. Gr. 2-4
SSJ1-20	Let's Visit Nova Scotia Gr. 2-4
SSJ1-34	Let's Visit Nunavut Gr. 2-4
SSJ1-17	Let's Visit Ontario Gr. 2-4
SSQ1-08	Let's Visit Ottawa Big Book Pkg 1-3
SSJ1-19	Let's Visit PEI Gr. 2-4
SSJ1-31	Let's Visit Québec Gr. 2-4
SSJ1-14	Let's Visit Saskatchewan Gr. 2-4
SSJ1-28	Let's Visit Yukon Gr. 2-4
SSN1-130	Life & Adv. of Santa Claus NS 7-8
SSB1-10	Life in a Pond Gr. 3-4
SSF1-30	Life in the Middle Ages Gr. 7-8
SSB1-103	Light & Sound Gr. 4-6
SSN1-219	Light in the Forest NS Gr. 7-8
SSN1-121	Light on Hogback Hill NS Gr. 4-6
SSN1-46	Lion, Witch & the Wardrobe NS 4-6
SSR1-51	Literature Response Forms Gr. 1-3
SSR1-52	Literature Response Forms Gr. 4-6
SSN1-28	Little House Big Woods NS 4-6
SSN1-233	Little House on the Prairie NS 4-6
SSN1-111	Little Women NS Gr. 7-8
SSN1-115	Live from the Fifth Grade NS 4-6
SSN1-141	Look Through My Window NS 4-6
SSN1-112	Look! Visual Discrimination Gr. P-1
SSN1-61	Lost & Found NS Gr. 4-6
SSN1-109	Lost in the Barrens NS Gr. 7-8
SSJ1-08	Lumbering Community Gr. 3-4
SSN1-167	Magic School Bus Gr. 1-3
SSN1-247	Magic Treehouse Gr. 1-3
SSB1-78	Magnets Gr. 3-5
SSD1-03	Making Sense of Our Senses K-1
SSN1-146	Mama's Going to Buy You a NS 4-6
SSB1-94	Mammals Gr. 1
SSB1-95	Mammals Gr. 2
SSB1-96	Mammals Gr. 3
SSB1-97	Mammals Gr. 5-6

Code #	Title and Grade
SSN1-160	Maniac Magee NS Gr. 4-6
SSA1-19	Mapping Activities & Outlines! 4-8
SSA1-17	Mapping Skills Gr. 1-3
SSA1-07	Mapping Skills Gr. 4-6
SST1-10A	March Gr. JK/SK
SST1-10B	March Gr. 1
SST1-10C	March Gr. 2-3
SSB1-57	Marvellous Marsupials Gr. 4-6
SSK1-01	Math Signs & Symbols Gr. 1-3
SSB1-116	Matter & Materials Gr. 1-3
SSB1-117	Matter & Materials Gr. 4-6
SSH1-03	Me, I'm Special! Gr. P-1
SSK1-16	Measurement Gr. 4-8
SSC1-02	Medieval Christmas Gr. 4-6
SSPC-09	Medieval Life B/W Pictures
SSC1-07	Merry Christmas Gr. P-K
SSK1-15	Metric Measurement Gr. 4-8
SSN1-13	Mice in Literature Gr. 3-5
SSB1-70	Microscopy Gr. 4-6
SSN1-180	Midnight Fox NS Gr. 4-6
SSN1-243	Midwife's Apprentice NS Gr. 4-6
SSJ1-07	Mining Community Gr. 3-4
SSK1-17	Money Talks – Cdn Gr. 3-6
SSK1-18	Money Talks – USA Gr. 3-6
SSB1-56	Monkeys & Apes Gr. 4-6
SSN1-43	Monkeys in Literature Gr. 2-4
SSN1-54	Monster Mania Gr. 4-6
SSN1-97	Mouse & the Motorcycle NS 4-6
SSN1-94	Mr. Poppers Penguins NS Gr. 4-6
SSN1-201	Mrs. Frisby & Rats NS Gr. 4-6
SSR1-13	Milti-Level Spelling Program Gr. 3-6
SSR1-26	Multi-Level Spelling USA Gr. 3-6
SSK1-31	Addition & Subtraction Drills 1-3
SSK1-32	Multiplication & Division Drills 4-6
SSK1-30	Multiplication Drills Gr. 4-6
SSA1-14	My Country! The USA! Gr. 2-4
SSN1-186	My Side of the Mountain NS 7-8
SSN1-58	Mysteries, Monsters & Magic Gr. 6-8
SSN1-37	Mystery at Blackrock Island NS 7-8
SSN1-80	Mystery House NS 4-6
SSN1-157	Nate the Great & Sticky Case NS 1-3
SSF1-23	Native People of North America 4-6
SSF1-25	New France Part 1 Gr. 7-8
SSF1-27	New France Part 2 Gr. 7-8
SSA1-10	New Zealand Gr. 4-8
SSN1-51	Newspapers Gr. 5-8
SSN1-47	No Word for Goodbye NS Gr. 7-8
SSPC-03	North American Animals B/W Pictures
SSF1-22	North American Natives Gr. 2-4
SSN1-75	Novel Ideas Gr. 4-6
SST1-06A	November JK/SK
SST1-06B	November Gr. 1
SST1-06C	November Gr. 2-3
SSN1-244	Number the Stars NS Gr. 4-6
SSY1-03	Numeration Gr. 1-3
SSPC-14	Nursery Rhymes B/W Pictures
SSN1-12	Nursery Rhymes Gr. P-1
SSN1-59	On the Banks of Plum Creek NS 4-6
SSN1-220	One in Middle Green Kangaroo NS 1-3
SSN1-145	One to Grow On NS Gr. 4-6
SSB1-27	Opossums Gr. 3-5
SSJ1-23	Ottawa Gr. 7-9
SSJ1-39	Our Canadian Governments Gr. 5-8
SSF1-14	Our Global Heritage Gr. 4-6
SSH1-12	Our Neighbourhoods Gr. 4-6
SSB1-72	Our Trash Gr. 2-3
SSB1-51	Our Universe Gr. 5-8
SSB1-86	Outer Space Gr. 1-2
SSA1-18	Outline Maps of the World Gr. 1-8
SSB1-67	Owls Gr. 4-6
SSN1-31	Owls in the Family NS Gr. 4-6
SSL1-02	Oxbridge Owl & The Library Gr. 4-6
SSB1-71	Pandas, Polar & Penguins Gr. 4-6
SSN1-52	Paperbag Princess NS Gr. 1-3
SSR1-11	Passion of Jesus: A Play Gr. 7-8
SSA1-12	Passport to Adventure Gr. 4-5
SSR1-06	Passport to Adventure Gr. 7-8
SSR1-04	Personal Spelling Dictionary Gr. 2-5
SSPC-29	Pets B/W Pictures
SSE1-03	Phantom of the Opera Gr. 7-9
SSN1-171	Phoebe Gilman Author Study Gr. 2-3
SSY1-06	Phonics Gr. 1-3
SSN1-237	Pierre Berton Author Study Gr. 7-8
SSN1-179	Pigman NS Gr. 7-8
SSN1-48	Pigs in Literature Gr. 2-4
SSN1-99	Pinballs NS Gr. 4-6
SSN1-60	Pippi Longstocking NS Gr. 4-6
SSF1-12	Pirates Gr. 4-6
SSK1-13	Place Value Gr. 4-6
SSB1-77	Planets Gr. 3-6
SSR1-74	Poetry Prompts Gr. 1-3
SSR1-75	Poetry Prompts Gr. 4-6

Code #	Title and Grade
SSB1-66	Popcorn Fun Gr. 2-3
SSB1-20	Porcupines Gr. 3-5
SSR1-55	Practice Manuscript Gr. Pk-2
SSR1-56	Practice Cursive Gr. 2-4
SSF1-24	Prehistoric Times Gr. 4-6
SSE1-01	Primary Music for Fall Gr. 1-3
SSE1-04	Primary Music for Spring Gr. 1-3
SSE1-07	Primary Music for Winter Gr. 1-3
SSJ1-47	Prime Ministers of Canada Gr. 4-8
SSK1-20	Probability & Inheritance Gr. 7-10
SSN1-49	Question of Loyalty NS Gr. 7-8
SSN1-26	Rabbits in Literature Gr. 2-4
SSB1-17	Raccoons Gr. 3-5
SSN1-207	Radio Fifth Grade NS Gr. 4-6
SSB1-52	Rainbow of Colours Gr. 4-6
SSN1-144	Ramona Quimby Age 8 NS 4-6
SSJ1-09	Ranching Community Gr. 3-4
SSY1-08	Reading for Meaning Gr. 1-3
SSN1-165	Reading Response Forms Gr. 1-3
SSN1-239	Reading Response Forms Gr. 4-6
SSN1-234	Reading with Arthur Gr. 1-3
SSN1-249	Reading with Canadian Authors 1-3
SSN1-200	Reading with Curious George Gr. 2-4
SSN1-230	Reading with Eric Carle Gr. 1-3
SSN1-251	Reading with Kenneth Oppel Gr. 4-6
SSN1-127	Reading with Mercer Mayer Gr. 1-2
SSN1-07	Reading with Motley Crew Gr. 2-3
SSN1-142	Reading with Robert Munsch 1-3
SSN1-06	Reading with the Super Sleuths 4-6
SSN1-08	Reading with the Ziggles Gr. 1
SST1-11A	Red Gr. JK/SK
SSN1-147	Refuge NS Gr. 7-8
SSC1-44	Remembrance Day Gr. 1-3
SSPC-23	Reptiles B/W Pictures
SSB1-42	Reptiles Gr. 4-6
SSN1-110	Return of the Indian NS Gr. 4-6
SSN1-225	River NS Gr. 7-8
SSE1-08	Robert Schuman, Composer Gr. 6-9
SSN1-83	Robot Alert NS Gr. 4-6
SSB1-65	Rocks & Minerals Gr. 4-6
SSN1-149	Romeo & Juliet NS Gr. 7-8
SSB1-88	Romping Reindeer Gr. K-3
SSN1-21	Rumplestiltskin NS Gr. 1-3
SSN1-153	Runaway Ralph NS Gr. 4-6
SSN1-103	Sadako & 1000 Paper Cranes NS 4-6
SSD1-04	Safety Gr. 2-4
SSN1-42	Sarah Plain & Tall NS Gr. 4-6
SSC1-34	School in September Gr. 4-6
SSPC-01	Sea Creatures B/W Pictures
SSB1-79	Sea Creatures Gr. 1-3
SSN1-64	Secret Garden NS Gr. 4-6
SSB1-90	Seeds & Weeds Gr. 2-3
SSY1-02	Sentence Writing Gr. 1-3
SST1-07A	September JK/SK
SST1-07B	September Gr. 1
SST1-07C	September Gr. 2-3
SSN1-30	Serendipity Series Gr. 3-5
SSC1-22	Shamrocks on Parade Gr. 1
SSC1-24	Shamrocks, Harps & Shillelaghs 3-4
SSR1-66	Shakespeare Shorts-Perf Arts Gr. 1-4
SSR1-67	Shakespeare Shorts-Perf Arts Gr. 4-6
SSR1-68	Shakespeare Shorts-Lang Arts Gr. 2-4
SSR1-69	Shakespeare Shorts-Lang Arts Gr. 4-6
SSB1-74	Sharks Gr. 4-6
SSN1-158	Shiloh NS Gr. 4-6
SSN1-84	Sideways Stories Wayside NS 4-6
SSN1-181	Sight Words Activities Gr. 1
SSB1-99	Simple Machines Gr. 4-6
SSN1-19	Sixth Grade Secrets 4-6
SSG1-04	Skill Building with Slates Gr. K-8
SSN1-118	Skinny Bones NS Gr. 4-6
SSB1-24	Skunks Gr. 3-5
SSN1-191	Sky is Falling NS Gr. 4-6
SSB1-83	Slugs & Snails Gr. 1-3
SSB1-55	Snakes Gr. 4-6
SST1-12A	Snow Gr. JK/SK
SST1-12B	Snow Gr. 1
SST1-12C	Snow Gr. 2-3
SSB1-76	Solar System Gr. 4-6
SSPC-44	South America B/W Pictures
SSA1-11	South America Gr. 4-6
SSB1-05	Space Gr. 2-3
SSR1-34	Spelling Blacklines Gr. 1
SSR1-35	Spelling Blacklines Gr. 2
SSR1-14	Spelling Gr. 1
SSR1-15	Spelling Gr. 2
SSR1-16	Spelling Gr. 3
SSR1-17	Spelling Gr. 4
SSR1-18	Spelling Gr. 5
SSR1-19	Spelling Gr. 6
SSR1-27	Spelling Worksavers #1 Gr. 3-5
SSM1-02	Spring Celebration Gr. 2-3

Code #	Title and Grade
SST1-01A	Spring Gr. JK/SK
SST1-01B	Spring Gr. 1
SST1-01C	Spring Gr. 2-3
SSM1-01	Spring in the Garden Gr. 1-2
SSB1-26	Squirrels Gr. 3-5
SSB1-112	Stable Structures & Mechanisms 3
SSG1-05	Steps in the Research Process 5-8
SSG1-02	Stock Market Gr. 7-8
SSN1-139	Stone Fox NS Gr. 4-6
SSN1-214	Stone Orchard NS Gr. 7-8
SSN1-01	Story Book Land of Witches Gr. 2-3
SSR1-64	Story Starters Gr. 1-3
SSR1-65	Story Starters Gr. 4-6
SSR1-73	Story Starters Gr. 1-6
SSY1-09	Story Writing Gr. 1-3
SSB1-111	Structures, Mechanisms & Motion 2
SSN1-211	Stuart Little NS Gr. 4-6
SSK1-29	Subtraction Drills Gr. 1-3
SSY1-05	Subtraction Gr. 1-3
SSY1-11	Successful Language Pract. Gr. 1-3
SSY1-12	Successful Math Practice Gr. 1-3
SSW1-09	Summer Learning Gr. K-1
SSW1-10	Summer Learning Gr. 1-2
SSW1-11	Summer Learning Gr. 2-3
SSW1-12	Summer Learning Gr. 3-4
SSW1-13	Summer Learning Gr. 4-5
SSW1-14	Summer Learning Gr. 5-6
SSN1-159	Summer of the Swans NS Gr. 4-6
SSZ1-02	Summer Olympics Gr. 4-6
SSM1-07	Super Summer Gr. 1-2
SSN1-18	Superfudge NS Gr. 4-6
SSA1-08	Switzerland Gr. 4-6
SSN1-20	T.V. Kid NS. Gr. 4-6
SSA1-15	Take a Trip to Australia Gr. 2-3
SSB1-102	Taking Off With Flight Gr. 1-3
SSN1-259	Tale of Despereaux Gr. 4-6
SSN1-55	Tales of the Fourth Grade NS 4-6
SSN1-188	Taste of Blackberries NS Gr. 4-6
SSK1-07	Teaching Math Through Sports 6-9
SST1-09A	Thanksgiving JK/SK
SST1-09C	Thanksgiving Gr. 2-3
SSN1-77	There's a Boy in the Girls... NS 4-6
SSN1-143	This Can't Be Happening NS 4-6
SSN1-05	Three Billy Goats Gruff NS Gr. 1-3
SSN1-72	Ticket to Curlew NS Gr. 4-6
SSN1-82	Timothy of the Cay NS Gr. 7-8
SSF1-32	Titanic Gr. 4-6
SSN1-222	To Kill a Mockingbird NS Gr. 7-8
SSN1-195	Toilet Paper Tigers NS Gr. 4-6
SSJ1-35	Toronto Gr. 4-8
SSH1-02	Toy Shelf Gr. P-K
SSPC-24	Toys B/W Pictures
SSN1-163	Traditional Poetry Gr. 7-10
SSH1-13	Transportation Gr. 4-6
SSW1-01	Transportation Snip Art
SSB1-03	Trees Gr. 2-3
SSA1-01	Tropical Rainforest Gr. 4-6
SSN1-56	Trumpet of the Swan NS Gr. 4-6
SSN1-81	Tuck Everlasting NS Gr. 4-6
SSN1-126	Turtles in Literature Gr. 1-3
SSN1-45	Underground to Canada NS 4-6
SSN1-27	Unicorns in Literature Gr. 3-5
SSJ1-44	Upper & Lower Canada Gr. 7-8
SSN1-192	Using Novels Canadian North Gr. 7-8
SSC1-14	Valentines Day Gr. 5-8
SSPC-45	Vegetables B/W Pictures
SSY1-01	Very Hungry Caterpillar NS 30/Pkg 1-3
SSF1-13	Victorian Era Gr. 7-8
SSC1-35	Victorian Christmas Gr. 5-8
SSF1-17	Viking Age Gr. 4-6
SSN1-206	War with Grandpa SN Gr. 4-6
SSB1-91	Water Gr. 2-4
SSN1-166	Watership Down NS Gr. 7-8
SSH1-16	Ways We Travel Gr. P-K
SSN1-101	Wayside Sch. Little Stranger NS 4-6
SSN1-76	Wayside Sch. is Falling Down NS 4-6
SSB1-60	Weather Gr. 4-6
SSN1-17	Wee Folk in Literature Gr. 3-5
SSPC-08	Weeds B/W Pictures
SSQ1-04	Welcome Back – Big Book Pkg 1-3
SSB1-73	Whale Preservation Gr. 5-8
SSH1-08	What is a Community? Gr. 2-4
SSH1-01	What is a Family? Gr. 2-3
SSH1-09	What is a School? Gr. 1-2
SSJ1-32	What is Canada? Gr. P-K
SSN1-79	What is RAD? Read & Discover 2-4
SSB1-62	What is the Weather Today? Gr. 2-4
SSN1-194	What's a Daring Detective NS 4-6
SSH1-10	What's My Number Gr. P-K
SSR1-02	What's the Scoop on Words Gr. 4-6
SSN1-73	Where the Red Fern Grows NS 7-8
SSN1-87	Where the Wild Things Are NS 1-3

Code #	Title and Grade
SSN1-187	Whipping Boy NS Gr. 4-6
SSN1-226	Who is Frances Rain? NS Gr. 4-6
SSN1-74	Who's Got Gertie & How...? NS 4-6
SSN1-131	Why did the Underwear ... NS 4-6
SSC1-28	Why Wear a Poppy? Gr. 2-3
SSJ1-11	Wild Animals of Canada Gr. 2-3
SSPC-07	Wild Flowers B/W Pictures
SSB1-18	Winter Birds Gr. 2-3
SSZ1-03	Winter Olympics Gr. 4-6
SSM1-04	Winter Wonderland Gr. 1
SSC1-01	Witches Gr. 3-4
SSN1-213	Wolf Island NS Gr. 1-3
SSE1-09	Wolfgang Amadeus Mozart 6-9
SSB1-23	Wolves Gr. 3-5
SSC1-20	Wonders of Easter Gr. 2
SSB1-35	World of Horses Gr. 4-6
SSB1-13	World of Pets Gr. 2-3
SSF1-26	World War II Gr. 7-8
SSN1-221	Wrinkle in Time NS Gr. 7-8
SSPC-02	Zoo Animals B/W Pictures
SSB1-08	Zoo Animals Gr. 1-2
SSB1-09	Zoo Celebration Gr. 3-4

Code #	Title and Grade

Code #	Title and Grade

Code #	Title and Grade